COMMUNITY AQUARIUMS

COMPLETELY ILLUSTRATED IN FULL COLOR

Terrestrial plants and the beautiful aquatic plants in this aquarium complement one another to provide sedate good looks. Photo courtesy Werther Paccagnella.

Cardinal tetras,
Paracheirodon axelrodi.
Photo by B. Kahl.

COMMUNITY AQUARIUMS

COMPLETELY ILLUSTRATED IN FULL COLOR

+ *The Red Phantom Tetra,* Megalamphodus sweglesi, *is a beautiful and charming little fish for community aquaria. Photo: H.–J. Richter.*

A COMPLETE INTRODUCTION TO

COMMUNITY AQUARIUMS

COMPLETELY ILLUSTRATED IN FULL COLOR

+ The ever–popular Harlequin Rasbora, Rasbora heteromorpha. *Photo: B. Kahl.*

Dr. Herbert R. Axelrod

Distributed in the UNITED STATES by T.F.H. Publications, Inc., 211 West Sylvania
Avenue, Neptune City, NJ 07753; in CANADA to the Pet Trade by H & L Pet Sup-
plies Inc., 27 Kingston Crescent, Kitchener, Ontario N2B 2T6; Rolf C. Hagen Ltd.,
3225 Sartelon Street, Montreal 382 Quebec; in CANADA to the Book Trade by
Macmillan of Canada (A Division of Canada Publishing Corporation), 164 Com-
mander Boulevard, Agincourt, Ontario M1S 3C7; in ENGLAND by T.F.H. Publica-
tions Limited, 4 Kier Park, Ascot, Berkshire SL5 7DS; in AUSTRALIA AND THE
SOUTH PACIFIC by T.F.H. (Australia) Pty. Ltd., Box 149, Brookvale 2100 N.S.W.,
Australia; in NEW ZEALAND by Ross Haines & Son, Ltd., 18 Monmouth Street,
Grey Lynn, Auckland 2 New Zealand; in SINGAPORE AND MALAYSIA by MPH
Distributors (S) Pte., Ltd., 601 Sims Drive, #03/07/21, Singapore 1438; in the
PHILIPPINES by Bio-Research, 5 Lippay Street, San Lorenzo Village, Makati Rizal;
in SOUTH AFRICA by Multipet Pty. Ltd., 30 Turners Avenue, Durban 4001. Pub-
lished by T.F.H. Publications Inc. Manufactured in the United States of America
by T.F.H. Publications, Inc.

Contents

Introduction

Ranking as America's second largest hobby, aquarium fishkeeping has outranked such popular pastimes as stamp collecting and gardening, and lies quite close to photography, with its 20,000,000 hobbyists.

Just why aquarium fishkeeping is so popular a hobby is difficul to explain. Like other popular hobbies, aquarium fishkeeping is a creative pastime. Many aquarists specialize in breeding colorful and exotic species from such far-away places as Thailand or Fernando Po. Still others seem to abhor the problems inherent in creating life and prefer to maintain a magnificent collection of different exotic fishes from all parts of the world, ranging in colors from the vibrant blue and scarlet red of the Cardinal Tetra to the olive drab of a *Corydoras* catfish. No one challenges the contention that just watching fishes swimming in an aquarium in your own living room can be relaxing, entertaining, and educational. Where else can the life cycles of fishes, plants, snails and other aquatic forms be observed under such ideal circumstances? Where else can children of all ages get their own answers to some of the most perplexing problems of life? Where else but among fishes can you find such varied techniques of reproduction such as egg-laying

*A community tank allows the aquarist to keep a variety of fishes in a single picturesque setting. Among the fishes inhabiting this community tank are Bleeding Heart Tetras (*Hyphessobrycon erythrostigma*), Angelfish (*Pterophyllum scalare*), and Silver Hatchetfishes (*Gasteropelecus sternicla*). Photo: B. Kahl.*

fishes which incubate their eggs in their mouth, or livebearing fishes which eat their own babies almost as soon as they are born unless you use a technique to save the young? Then there are fishes which jump out of the water to lay their eggs on the aquarium's rim...and there are still others which inject their eggs into the bodies of living clams. Perhaps the most interesting breeding technique is that of the famous Siamese Fighting Fish, *Betta splendens*, which makes a nest of bubbles floating on the surface, and then spits his spawn into this floating nest to keep them near the oxygen rich water they need to develop. Yes, all of these techniques are easily observed in your own home aquarium, and this is just one phase of the interesting hobby of aquarium fishkeeping.

How to Start in the Hobby

It is almost academic that since you are reading this book about aquarium fishes, you must be interested in the hobby. Perhaps you are contemplating whether or not to start? Or, having just begun, perhaps you are looking for further avenues of aquarium adventure? One of the greatest appeals of aquarium fishkeeping for the beginner is that it is possible to become a hobbyist with a minimum investment of money. Even a small aquarium of about five gallons capacity is large enough with which to begin. In it you need only a small bunch plant of *Cabomba, Anacharis* or *Myriophyllum* or, easier yet, plastic plants, to set the stage.

live plants for the beginner since they will not die while he is learning more about other aspects of his hobby.

How to Use This Book

This is a guide book made to take with you when you go to the pet shop looking for new additions to your aquarium collection. The most popular aquarium fishes are illustrated in this book, and with most illustrations are captions which give such useful information as the popular and scientific name of the fish, its range, and its size. Those fish whose captions are preceded by a plus sign (+) are community aquarium fishes and will generally

Simple but efficient: this tank set up with power filter and heater is sparsely furnished but very attractive.

These aquarium plants serve several purposes. One purpose is to decorate the aquarium and make it a thing of beauty. Plants also serve as hiding places for timid or young fish. Many fishes need a bit of vegetable matter in their diet, and aquarium plants serve this purpose ideally. Plastic plants, however, are better than

get along well with other fishes. Remember, though, that almost every fish will eat "bite-sized" fish, even their own offspring. Do not put small fishes in tanks with very large fish. Some captions are preceded by a minus sign (−), indicating fishes which are not suitable for mixed tanks. Such fishes are either extremely carnivorous or aggressive, or have other bad faults. An exclamation point (!) marks fishes which grow too large for the community aquarium. There are very few of these, as even large fish seldom grow to their full size in aquaria.

Wherever possible, the illustrations show the mature, breeding colors of male and female of the species. Almost without exception, young males are colored like mature females and usually have the secondary sex characteristics of mature females. Keep this in mind if you try to select pairs of young fish. The "female" you chose may be a male in a few weeks!

The immense community aquarium at one side of this spacious and airy room blends in well with the terrestrial plants.

The Livebearers

The Livebearers

The fishes with which the beginning aquarist usually starts are the livebearers. These are fishes which deliver their young alive, not in the usual egg form. Though there is some controversy about exactly how much the mother fish contributes to the development of her internally fertilized eggs, it is certainly not a mammalian relationship and there is probably little physical connection between the developing eggs and the body of the mother. As a result, most of the livebearing fishes are called "ovoviviparous" while the egglayers are called "oviparous." A mammal, excepting the duckbilled platypus, is "viviparous."

The Swordtails

Of all the livebearers, the most colorful and among the most common are the *Xiphophorus* species. Interestingly, the Greek scientific name *"Xiphophorus"* means "to bear a sword" but this name was not given to the Swordtail because the males have the sword-like extension on the tail fins. A close examination of the male Swordtail will indicate that his anal fin is not fan-shaped like a female Swordtail's, but has developed into a seemingly solid spike. What has happened is that the individual fin rays have fused to form a sex organ through which the male is able to fertilize the female internally by "shooting" packets of sperm into her genital pore. The female has the ability to store this sperm for several months, at least, and to fertilize future developing eggs without any additional assistance from the male. Often a beginner wonders how a female Swordtail, having been separated from a male for months, suddenly starts to grow swollen about her abdomen and shortly thereafter gives birth to a brood of youngsters. The gestation period of the Swordtails is about a month, varying a few days, more or less, with the temperature of the water and the amount of light they receive (in terms of hours per day). Optimum temperature is 75 to 78°. The young Swordtails, usually 50 to 100 in number, are independent of their parents immediately after birth. As a matter of fact, it is usual that some Swordtails will actually search out and eat their own fry! Your petshop sells mechanical devices which prevent Swordtail mothers with cannibalistic tendencies from devouring their own young. These "breeding traps" are usually small plastic aquariums which hang inside the main aquarium. The bottom is slotted so the fry fall through as they are delivered, and the female is unable to go after them since the slots are too small for her girth.

Swordtails are available in many colors and patterns. The natural color of a wild Swordtail, which is still found in many parts of Mexico and Central America, is a drab green, though some races show a bit of red. But none is found with the unbelievable colors and patterns which have been developed in genetics laboratories and fish farms. In the usual Swordtail, you can find individuals which are jet black, green, brick red, blood red, velvet red, gold, yellow (albino), and red albino. But, through the efforts of the late Dr. Myron Gordon, a famous geneticist who used Swordtails and Platies to study the genetics of cancer, new forms were developed which had black lips, dorsal fins, caudal fins and pectoral fins. These forms

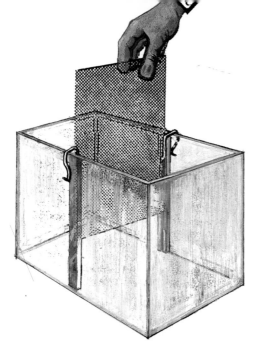

Fishes that have to be separated during quarantine periods or as part of a pre-spawning routine can be housed together in the same tank if the tank is partitioned; inexpensive partitions are available at shops selling aquarium equipment.

Gordon called "Wagtail Swordtails" because when the fish would swim, the black tails looked as if they were "wagging." By other breeding experiments, Gordon was able to develop fish with black only in the lower area of their bodies, and these he called "Tuxedo Swordtails." Eventually, by careful selective breeding, Gordon and some commercial hatcheries were able to develop Tuxedo Swordtails with all of the body colors previously mentioned. There are even Tuxedo Wagtail Swordtails! But don't think that only great scientists and commercial breeders are able to develop new strains. Far from it! In Gardena, California, Mrs. Thelma Simpson noticed a few Swordtails which had longer dorsal fins than the normal fish. She kept breeding those Swordtails with each other, always selecting those with the

longest dorsal fins until she had developed a strain of Swordtail which bears the name "Simpson Hifin Swordtail." It only took a few years before they were bred in all colors, with "tuxedos" and "wagtails," too! Perhaps YOU might develop a strain of your own.

Dr. Gordon wrote many scientific papers and a few popular booklets about Swordtails and Platies, and if you are interested in breeding these fishes for new color varieties, you should consult the T.F.H. book *Genetics for Aquarists*. Isn't it amazing that all of these beautiful color varieties came about from the common Green Swordtail?

But where there is such a strongly inbred strain of Swordtails, and where Swordtails so freely interbreed with other color varieties of Swordtail and

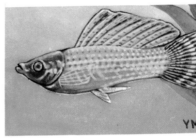

Liberty Molly, male. Poecilia (formerly Mollienesia) sphenops.

Albino Molly, male. Poecilia (formerly Mollienesia) latipinna.

This community tank is set up as an all-livebearer tank. It houses Mollies, Guppies, Swordtails, and Platies. All of these fishes could be kept together in a community aquarium, but for maximum good development members of each different species would be better off in a tank of their own. The Mollies, for example, are a little more demanding in their requirements and generally do better when maintained alone.

Male (left) and female Black Molly, Poecilia *(formerly* Mollienesia) latipinna.

Platy, you are often quite surprised at the offspring that your female may produce. It is only through a constant inbreeding of a Red Swordtail to other Red Swordtails that you have a strain of pure Red Swordtails. It is very common for Red Swordtails to have Green Swordtail babies...even along with her Red Swordtail babies. Thus, if you want to breed a certain color variety of Swordtail, you must maintain each variety in its own aquarium and be careful that one doesn't jump into another tank, for Swordtails are excellent jumpers. It is the usual practice to have a glass cover or a reflector hood on every aquarium, not only to prevent accidental matings, but to keep fishes inside their tanks, and dust, dirt and children's hands out!

Certain colors dominate over others in Swordtails. The most prized fishes are those with the most intense coloration. As yet, Blue Swordtails are a rarity, while deep velvet blood Red Swordtails are the most sought after color variety. The least expensive are the Green Swordtails, while the medium priced Red Tuxedo Swordtails are becoming very popular.

Haphazard breeding results in various types of Swordtails which are sometimes called "Hybrid Swordtails." They are the least desirable because their color pattern has not been genetically fixed and their offspring are nondescript in pattern and generally not especially appealing.

The Platies

Very closely related to the Swordtails are the Platyfishes. So closely interbred are the Platies and Swordtails that it can safely be generalized that most Platies now available at petshops have Swordtails some place in their ancestry. The reverse is true, also. Due to constant inbreeding by commercial fish

+ *Red Tuxedo Platies (*Xiphophorus maculatus*) are one of the most popular of the color varieties of platies. Like other strains, this one surely has swordtail blood mixed in somewhere in its background. Photo: B. Kahl.*

+ Upper Photo: *The Gold Indent Comet Platy has this unusual caudal fin shape in addition to the comet pattern. Photo: H. Linke.* Lower Photo: *The Sunburst Platy seen here is a relatively new strain. It has become popular in a very short period of time. Photo: B. Kahl.*

breeders, Platies and Swordtails are found with nearly identical colors and color patterns. There are Wagtail Platies and Tuxedo Platies, counterparts are to be found in the Swordtail group. But while we have very beautiful Blue Platies, no one has yet established a strain of Blue Swordtails. And, conversely, while Green Swordtails are the most common, there are no Green Platies to be had! Wild Platies are available today only in genetics laboratories and in their native Mexico and Central America. This is understandable since they are not beautiful fishes. They are

Some sellers of tropical fish add oxygen to the plastic bag in which the fish will be transported, thereby providing an extra measure of safety.

colorless, and at best have a little black in the tail or caudal peduncle, to break the monotony of their plain-colored body. All of the color varieties of Platies have been developed through cultivation.

If you examine the Gold Wagtail Platy, you will discover that, except for the thickened anal fin of the male (called a *gonopodium*) they are almost identical to the female Gold Wagtail Swordtail. The Swordtail is a bit longer and

+ *This is a beautiful gold "Salt & Pepper" Platy. Photo: Dr. H. Grier.*

more slender, but there would be no problem in breeding a male Gold Wagtail Platy with a female Gold Wagtail Swordtail, or vice versa. But take a variety that doesn't exist in both Swordtails and Platies, such as the Bleeding Heart Platy, and you have another problem. There are no Bleeding Heart Swordtails and if you cross a Bleeding Heart Platy with, say, a Gold Swordtail, you get Green Swordtails and some other nondescript fishes with very short swords on their tails, or with no swords at all. But this doesn't prevent the interbreeding of Platies with Swordtails, and theoretically, anyway, there is no reason why someday we won't have Swordtails and Platies in every color of the rainbow.

Some Platies which have a dark crescent-shaped marking on their tails are called "Moons." In the vocabulary of the fish breeder, a "Moon" is usually a larger type Platy with the marking in the tail. This marking, by the way, was found in wild Platies, and it varies in intensity in nearly every

Platyfish, both cultured and wild.

Xiphophorus helleri is not the only Swordtail in the genus *Xiphophorus*; there are two much less colorful species, *X. montezumae,* which has a short, spike tail and *X. pygmaeus* which has no sword on its tail at all. *X. maculatus (maculatus* means *spotted* and refers to the spots in the wild specimens) is not the only species of Platyfish. The Platy Variatus, *X. variatus,* is a platy which is quite different than *X. maculatus.* It differs in that while Swordtail males and females are colored alike, and the other Platies are also sexually indistinguishable on the basis of color alone, Platy Variatus sexes are quite different. The wild male is intensely colored and the female is drab. It has only been recently that females with color have been cultivated in the fish farms in Florida, and this variety, the SUNSET, is presently very popular.

Not only are Platy Variatus hardier than other Platies and Swordtails, but different color

+ *The Platy Variatus,* Xiphophorus variatus, *is quite a stunning fish, even in those strains that do not vary tremendously from wild stock. Photo: B. Kahl.*

varieties have been established. First, there is an albino Platy Variatus, the first Platy which has been albinized. Other strains include the Red-tail Platy Variatus, where the male has a red tail and the female's tail is colorless. A bright Yellow-tail Platy Variatus has also been developed; but here too the tail of the female is colorless. In the Sunset Platy Variatus we find a strain where both male and female are intensely colored, though the males are inclined to be a bit more colorful especially in strains which are not carefully culled of off-color individuals.

While it is very simple to interbreed between the various strains of Platy Variatus, it is not so easy to cross them with Swordtails and other strains of Platies, though it has been done on occasion. Without getting too technical here, a clarification of terms may be useful. Within a genus, hybrids are possible, but most often sterile. For example a jackass and a mare produce the famous Missouri mule. Individual varieties and strains within a species may be cross mated, and some fertile young should be produced. A variety of a species is different enough to be readily recognized, but has no trouble breeding with other varieties; and a strain breeds true for color and appearance.

The Guppies

Pehaps the most prolific fish to be found in aquaria all over the world is the Guppy. The common strains are very inexpensive, hardy, and omnivorous, eating everything and anything offered to them. They are ideal fish for the beginner, and their color patterns, fin shapes and size are so variable that many advanced hobbyists restrict their aquaria to Guppies alone.

In the Guppy is to be found a most interesting fish. Originally discovered in Caracas, Venezuela, it has been introduced all over the world to help control mosquitos, for the Guppy can live

+ *The common Guppy (*Poecilia reticulata*). The males are the more colorful of the sexes and possess a gonopodium (modified anal fin). There is an almost infinite variety of patterns in a tankful of common Guppies. Photo: B. Kahl.*

in the smallest pool of water, under the most adverse conditions, and still thrive and breed. Thus, when a newcomer to the hobby has to select a fish with which to begin the hobby, the Guppy is usually the choice.

Of the Guppy, until very recently, it would be safe to say that two males identically colored didn't exist; while two females differently colored didn't exist. Now, under the skillful hands of famous fish breeders all over the world, strains of Guppies have been produced wherein all

+ *Although common Guppy females are virtually colorless, many of the fancy varieties have females that develop larger and more colorful fins. This fancy Guppy female is giving birth to a living youngster. Photo: R. Zukal.*

+ A male Black Fantail Guppy. Photo: A. Noznov.

males are identically colored, and females differ from strain to strain. No one has yet produced a female with colors as intense as those of a male, but by using some of the "color foods" and additives available at every petshop, it is possible to bring out colors in female Guppies heretofore deemed impossible.

If Guppies are well fed, and they eat any of the dry foods sold for Guppies and all tropical fish, chances are that they will not cannibalize their fry.

Considering that they have as many as 100 young at a time, you can readily understand why literature has referred to them as "The Millions Fish." Real satisfaction comes from breeding Guppies with long, highly colored tails and dorsal fins and Guppy Societies have shows every year where Guppy breeders compete

with each other for the most colorful Guppy with the longest tail and dorsal fin.

Paul Hahnel, a master cabinet maker by profession, is generally credited with the development of the first recognizable strain of fancy long-tailed Guppies. He started his serious efforts in the early nineteen fifties and by 1955 had won just about every international award that Guppy breeders strive for.

The Mollies

The genus *Mollienesia* (now considered to be a subgenus of *Poecilia*) contains fishes that have become very desirable both because of the intense black strains and the striking fin development which have been developed from the normal nondescript wild fishes. Mollies are found in freshwater, brackish water and even in the Atlantic Ocean from Florida to Texas. Though most of the wild forms are plain greenish silver, there are individuals which have been found heavily mottled with black.

Under the skillful hands of the fish farmer, many strains have been developed, from the giant Orange-dorsal Sailfin Molly, where the male has a huge dorsal fin tipped with orange, to the fish which is called the "Yucatan Molly" where the male's dorsal is no larger than the female's.

Mollies freely interbreed with each other and there are some very interesting strains. The Perma-Black Molly is a Black Molly whose fry are born black and stay black. Many strains of Black Molly have black babies which turn gray after a few weeks and gradually turn black again as they mature, in about four months. These fish are never as intensely black as the Perma-Black strain. The Sailfin Black Mollies, on the other hand, show various dorsal fin developments, but only one male in a thousand develops into a really handsome fish so much in demand. It is virtually impossible to raise Mollies with huge dorsals in the home aquarium. All tank-raised Mollies have small dorsals and are dwarfed; but in the huge pools in Florida where most Mollies are bred, all of the male Sailfin Mollies have an opportunity to develop large dorsals if the genetic potential is there. No one has suitably explained why the dorsal doesn't fully develop in home-raised fish.

Though Mollies are very hardy, they do require hard, alkaline water (pH 7.6 to 8.6). If they are not properly maintained they quickly become ill and have a

+ *Fancy Guppies are excellent fishes for community aquaria, but be careful not to mix them with fast–moving fishes that may nip their fins, such as Tiger Barbs. Photo: M. Gilroy.*

+ Above: *The Black Sailfin Molly* (Poecilia latipinna) *is one of the most popular strains of molly. A little salt in the water and a diet heavy in vegetable matter are strongly recommended.* Below: *The Marbled Molly (Poecilia* latipinna) *is a mixture of the black and silver varieties. Some marble strains are quite attractive, while others are less so. Photos: Andre Roth.*

characteristic disease known as the "shimmies." This disease is usually initiated by a sudden drop in water temperature, either while the fish are being shipped from Florida to the neighborhood petshop, or in the home aquarium where a faulty heater is to blame.

The treatment is to raise the temperature of the water to about 80°F. with an aquarium heater, thermostatically controlled and use a neutravitalizer stone to "harden" the water.

There are other strains of Mollies, as well as still other species. While the Orange-dorsal Sailfin Molly is *Poecilia (Mollienesia) latipinna,* there is yet another type of Sailfin Molly known as *Poecilia (Mollienesia) velifera.* This latter species, called the Green Sailfin Molly, occurs in the wild and has resisted the best efforts of commercial breeders to develop a black variety. The most beautiful specimens are those caught in the wild.

In the early 1960's a Chinese fishbreeder in Singapore discovered among his usual Black Sailfin Mollies one with a longer tail. It also had longer ventral and pectoral fins. By selective breeding he was able to fix the strain which resulted in the Lyretailed Mollies, a very beautiful strain. In Florida under more favorable conditions, this fish was crossed with the Sphenops Molly, *Poecilia (Mollienesia) sphenops,* and a whole new group of Mollies was initiated.

The Sphenops Molly, like the Platy Variatus, has a completely different genetic makeup than the other Mollies. Whereas, except for the difference in dorsal fin size in the other Mollies, the sexes are very similar, in the Sphenops we find the males are intensely colored, with flaming red and orange tails in many cases, while the females, at best, show only a hint of color in their tails. The dorsal fin of the male Sphenops is also larger and more shapely than the female's. All species of Mollies require the same care. All are vegetarians, too, so live aquarium plants are practically a necessity with these fishes.

The Halfbeaks

Not all livebearing fishes are from the New World, though certainly the most colorful species which are suitable for home aquaria do come from the Americas. From the mainland of Asia and some of the Indonesian islands comes the interesting Wrestling Halfbeak. Here we have a fish which is essentially colorless, though some forms do have a bit of red in their tails. It is appreciated by hobbyists because of its pointed

— *The Wrestling Halfbeak* (Dermogenys pusillus) *is mostly colorless, although some other forms (species?) may have red or yellow colored unpaired fins. Photo: B. Kahl.*

mouth with jutting lower jaw and fighting habits.

The Wrestling Halfbeak is, first of all, a livebearer. It would have little place in the aquarium if that were all it had to offer, for it is difficult to maintain without live foods in its diet. But two males, when they encounter each other scanning the surface for food, might lock jaws and wrestle, until one breaks the grip and dives for cover, never again to cruise the surface for food while the victor is in the same area. In Thailand there are fish-fights which feature this species, with heavy wagers bet on the outcome. Of course Thailand is also the home of the Siamese fighting fish also called the Betta, and more about that later.

The Mosquitofishes

In nearly every coastal ditch from Charleston, South Carolina, to Buenos Aires, Argentina, are to be found a score of different species of livebearing fishes. These are colorless fishes which are rarely appreciated in the home aquarium because they are vicious, hard to keep alive, and demanding in their diets. Fortunately, they serve humanity well, for their natural diet is composed mainly of mosquito pupae, mosquito larvae and the larvae of other aquatic insects. When it was discovered that a tiny fish known as *Heterandria formosa,* from South Carolina, could eat its own weight in mosquito larvae every day, malariologists cultivated them and introduced them to stagnant streams and pools all over the world. Tropical fish hobbyists use them in their outdoor garden pools for the same purpose and occasionally they are to be found in home aquaria, especially in tanks where there are fishes which restrict their activity to the bottom like Catfish and Loaches, for the Mosquitofish always stays on the top.

Of the many, many species of Mosquitofish, only a few are kept in aquaria. One of these is the popular *Gambusia affinis.* Today, the word *Gambusino* (which

+ *Heterandria formosa is often known as the "Least Killifish" even though it is a poeciliid livebearer. This attractive little fish is common over much of the southeastern U.S. Photo: M. Brembach.*

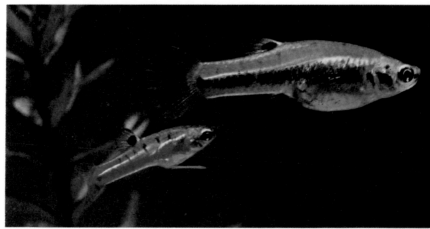

+ *One of the Limias,* Poecilia nigrofasciata. *Photo: Dr. S. Frank.*

actually means "nothing"), refers to any kind of small livebearing fish which eats mosquitos. The *Gambusia* sometimes available have been intensively cultivated and there are several interesting color varieties available. The normal *Gambusia affinis* is merely a silver fish. Cultivated varieties, with various mottled patterns, are available. Though rare, all-black *Gambusia* are available from time to time; the strain is far from being fixed.

Males are usually much smaller than females and both are colored identically. It is not unheard of for a female to eat all the males in the same aquarium with her if she hasn't had live foods for a while.

Since Mosquitofish are carnivorous by nature, it isn't wise to maintain them with smaller fishes unless they are well fed with Tubifex worms, frozen brine shrimp or other forms of live foods. Gambusia are not recommended for the beginner.

The Limias
Though much larger than the usual Mosquitofishes, the Limias are livebearers which serve the same function and do a superior job of mosquito extermination. Most petshops carry one or two species of *Limia,* though they are falling into disfavor since such colorful strains of Swordtails, Platies and Mollies are available. Vacationers in Haiti, Jamaica and other West Indian Islands can easily catch their own!

One of the thrills of aquarium fishkeeping is to capture and bring back your own specimens from some of the tropical and semi-tropical parts to which you may travel. In nearly every stream in the West Indies, including the Virgin Islands, Puerto Rico, and northern South America, a large net will produce hundreds of *Limia* with just a little help from a friend. Spread the seine across a stream. Enter the stream about ten feet from where the net is spread and chase the fish into the seine, lifting it quickly to prevent their escape. By keeping the fishes in a heavy plastic bag, with plenty of water, you can usually manage to bring back enough

+ *The Red-tailed Goodeid* (Xenotoca eiseni) *is generally peaceful with other fishes as long as they are not too small. The water should be relatively hard. Note the characteristic notch in the anal fin of this male. Photo: H.-J. Richter.*

fishes for your friends, as well as yourself. It is satisfying to point to a fish swimming in your living room in the dead of winter, and remarking: "I caught that one in Haiti."

The Limias freely interbreed if members of their opposite sex, same species, are not available. The resultant crosses are usually sterile, though, so there hasn't been too much cross-breeding of this genus. Keep your Limias in the largest aquarium possible. They require about one gallon of water per fish, with plenty of vegetation.

Whereas most of the

– *The Celebes Halfbeak* (Nomorhamphus liemi) *is a livebearer that, although relatively peaceful, is best kept by itself. Live foods are recommended. Photo: H.-J. Richter.*

+ *Though not always brightly colored, wild livebearers are becoming quite popular with specialist breeders. This is* Girardinus metallicus. *Photo: B. Kahl.*

Mosquitofishes previously discussed are to be found between Florida on the north and Trinidad on the south, there are some species which are found only in Brazil and further south. *Micropoecilia branneri* has sometimes been called the "Brazilian Guppy." The males are tiny and variegated in coloration, much like the male Guppy. These fish are found inland, sometimes a thousand miles from the ocean. The other Mosquitofishes, though they prefer fresh water, are also found very close to the ocean, and have been shown to have great tolerance for brackish water.

Micropoecilia branneri is one of the oddities of the aquarium world, especially for collectors. This fish is found in the same streams and lakes as fishes which could swallow them in one gulp. Yet they are always found in great numbers, always hugging the first few inches of the shore line, always healthy and active. As the pools and streams dry up, these

fishes are the last to perish. They are fast swimmers and very difficult to catch, yet they are always in full view, for they never stray from the surface of the water. Even fish-eating birds are unable to catch them!

There is one species *Cnesterodon decemmaculatus*, found in Brazil, Paraguay, Uruguay and Argentina, which is equally at home in puddles so small that they contain less than 5 gallons of muddy, dirty water from a barnyard drainage, and also in huge ditches in the mountains which are covered by ice three months of the year. Yet, even with great care, these fish often die in a few days when kept under seemingly perfect conditions in the home aquarium!

These are some of the problems which fascinate the advanced hobbyist. Perhaps you will be one of those who are destined to give the world the answer to some of the mysteries of aquarium life.

The Tetras or Characins

The Tetras or Characins

One of the largest families of fishes, and one of the most interesting for the aquarist, is the family Characidae. Commonly called Characins, or Tetras, these fishes are found in North, Central and South America, as well as Africa. They range from the bizarre, ferocious Piranhas, the so-called Man-eaters of the Amazon to the tiny, gaudily colorful Cardinal Tetra. Nearly all of the Tetras you will find in petshops today come from Peru, Brazil or British Guiana. But every year more and more new varieties are found: one more beautiful than the next!

As a group, Tetras have certain common characteristics. They all have teeth, though some of the teeth are invisible to the naked eye. Most have an extra fin behind the dorsal fin on the back, known as the *adipose fin*. This fin has no rays in it and is sometimes called the "fatty fin." All Tetras subsist well on live foods, and many of the smaller varieties, especially those in the genera *Hyphessobrycon, Hemigrammus* and *Cheirodon* can get along with regular dried or freeze-dried aquarium foods and some frozen brine shrimp now and then.

American Tetras

The Tetras are the favorites of the author, and he has been very successful in finding many new species in the streams of the Brazilian Amazon jungle. Among the most beautiful are *Paracheirodon axelrodi* and the Black Neon, *Hyphessobrycon herbertaxelrodi*. According to the Rules of the Commission on Zoological Nomenclature, an international body of scientists which makes sure that the same fish doesn't have two names, a fish must be described scientifically in a publication. This

+ *The Cardinal Tetra,* Paracheirodon axelrodi, *is undoubtedly one of the most beautiful freshwater fishes in the world. Though it can adapt to other water conditions, it prefers soft, acid water. Photo: H.–J. Richter.*

+ *The Flame Tetra*, Hyphessobrycon flammeus, *is a species with much to recommend it: it is very peaceful, hardy, and easy to breed. Photo: B. Kahl.*

description, usually accompanied by a drawing or photograph, shows how many rows of scales the fish has, how large it is in proportion to the eye and other parts of the body (a fish can be 6.8 eye lengths long, for example), how deep it is in proportion to its head, the number of rays in its various fins, its color pattern, etc.

The describer also gives the fish a name. A scientist does not name a fish after himself, but may name it after the discoverer, the place where it is found, or after a Latin or Greek term or word which best describes it. Thus, *H. serpae* is named after the town Serpa on the Amazon. *H. bifasciatus* means two-banded, while *H. heterorhabdus* means different banded.

The popular names given to the fish are not necessarily proper in many cases. *H. flammeus* is often called the Tetra from Rio, for that was where it was found, though some call it the Flame Tetra, since that is what *flammeus* means in English. The very beautiful Neon Tetra, *Paracheirodon innesi*, was named to honor William T. Innes, a printer and author of fish literature and it is one of the most popular of all Tetras, but since that time the Cardinal Tetra, because it has more red and more blue and grows larger, has become more popular. Another Neon Tetra, *Paracheirodon simulans*, is very similar to the *P. innesi*. It was discovered in Brazil (it is not illustrated here since it looks so much like *P. innesi*).

All Tetras require an aquarium which allows them plenty of swimming space. Their usual temperature requirements are 74 to 84°F., though some species, especially those from Argentina and southern Brazil can stand short periods at a lower temperature. Most of the small

+ *Though not exactly a show–stopper,* Pristella maxillaris *is quite attractive with its red tail. Photo: B. Kahl.*

Tetras get along well together, especially Tetras belonging to the same genus. The pretty *Pristella maxilaris* from Trinidad and Venezuela is peaceful enough to get along with any other Tetra which isn't too large. The *Pristella* is one of the few Tetras which is also available in the albino form. Perhaps, by closely examining your own fishes, you might find a Tetra which has no black in it whatsoever. This would be an albino. All albinos have pink eyes, devoid of black pigment.

Another interesting aquarium paradox is the Golden Tetra, which the author discovered in British Guiana and named *Hemigrammus armstrongi* in

+ Hemigrammus sp. aff. rodwayi. *This tetra is very similar to that sold as the Gold Tetra in the hobby. Photo: A. Norman.*

honor of his friend, Joseph Armstrong. After collecting some beautiful Golden Tetras and taking exceptional pains to "bring 'em back alive", it was very disappointing to discover that all of their offspring were silver and had no trace of the beautiful golden color of their parents. In the second generation there were some golden specimens but not enough to make tank-breeding this species profitable. Returning to British Guiana, the author couldn't find any silver specimens at all!! The reason, it was later revealed, is that the gold specimens result from parasites.

If you examine the Tetras which have been illustrated thus far, you will discover that all have basically the same laterally-compressed shape. But there are some Tetras which have a rounded, pencil-like shape and these are called the Pencilfishes.

The genera *Poecilobrycon* and *Nannostomus* contain the most beautiful South American Pencilfishes. They are all very peaceful, delicate and slow-moving, especially when compared with the ceaseless swimming of many Tetras. Due to their small mouths, Pencilfishes must be offered fine-grained fish foods; newly hatched brine shrimp is the best. Don't keep your Pencilfishes with other "bullies." They do best alone, and their quiet, serene ways make them ideal fish for the small aquarium since they do not require much oxygen and get along nicely in an aquarium without an air pump or filter.

The breeding habits of Pencilfishes are about the same as that of the other Tetras. The pairs dash quickly into the plant thickets and spray their eggs, haphazardly, into the fine leaves. The only attention they pay to

+ *Nannostomus marginatus, one of the small and peaceful Pencilfishes. Photo by H. J. Richter.*

them is the dubious compliment of eating them! The spawning dance is a beautiful sight to see. The Pencilfishes line their bodies next to each other and, with widespread fins, tremble while maneuvering tightly together into the thickets. Their eggs, as with most Tetras, hatch in a day or two, depending upon the temperature. The newborn fry require newly hatched brine shrimp or some infusorians, such as *Paramecium*.

Closely related to the Pencilfishes are the *Copellas.* They jump very readily and have a very diverse breeding pattern. *Pyrrhulina rachoviana,* for example, spawns like a Cichlid by depositing her eggs on a leaf. The male then tends the eggs by posing on top of them and fanning them with a flow of water. The eggs will hatch in about 24 hours and if the pair aren't removed, they will probably eat

their own babies. The commercial breeder removes the leaf and hatches the eggs over a stream of air bubbles or a gentle flow from a water pump.

In contrast to *Pyrrhulina rachoviana,* we have *Copeina arnoldi.* This Tetra, called the Spraying Characin, has a unique breeding habit. The pair select an overhanging leaf which lies an inch or two above the surface of the water. Then, after several false starts, they lock fins and jump out of the water onto the leaf they selected. Utilizing their fins to form miniature suction cups, they cling to the leaf for a second or two, deposit their spawn and fall back into the water. This continues until hundreds of eggs are laid on the leaf. (If a leaf isn't available, they use a rock, or, in the aquarium, they may use anything hanging over the water, even a fluorescent tube.) But their care of the eggs

+ *The Hatchetfishes are great jumpers and their aquaria should be kept tightly covered. Shown is a trio of Marble Hatchetfish,* Carnegiella strigata strigata. *Photo: Dr. Herbert R. Axelrod.*

+ *One of the Bloodfin Tetras,* Aphyocharax rubripinnis. *These active, hardy fish will eat almost any foods, and a school of them is a great asset to any community tank. Photo: B. Kahl.*

doesn't stop there. The male then utilizes his longer tail and dorsal fin to splash water onto the eggs periodically so they stay moist. When the eggs hatch, after a few days, the fry simply fall into the water and swim away!

The Red-spotted Copeina, *Copeina guttata,* though very closely related to *Copeina arnoldi,* has completely different spawning habits. The pair, once they begin their spawning ritual of dancing and prancing in front of each other with outspread fins, selects a small clearing on the bottom of the aquarium. Then the pair begins to dig a depression in the sand by "biting" the bottom and spitting the sand around the sides and by forcing their bodies into the gravel to make the depression deeper. The female then lays the eggs in this depression and both parents guard them against intruders. As soon as the eggs

begin to develop, the male chases the female away and continues fanning the eggs, in typical cichlid fashion and similar to *Pyrrhulina rachoviana.* These eggs take about two days to hatch, and the male usually ignores the fry after they are free-swimming. The spawn is large, numbering about 250 eggs. In contrast to this behavior is the beautiful-scaled Characin, *Copeina callolepis.* This species spawns on a leaf, similar to *Pyrrhulina rachoviana,* but once the eggs are laid, the parents should be removed or they might eat their fry. The spawns are small, numbering about 50 eggs. The eggs hatch in a day, but the young must lie on the bottom for a few days until they absorb the very heavy yolk sacs.

Closely related to the Pencilfishes are the Tetras of the genus *Anostomus.* No popular

+ *Striped Headstander* (Anostomus anostomus). *Photo: H.-J. Richter.*

+ *Congo Tetra* (Phenacogrammus interruptus). *Photo: A. Roth.*

+ *Six–barred Distichodus* (Distichodus sexfasciatus). *Photo: G. Wolfsheimer.*

name has been given to these fishes, but certainly Cigarfishes would not be improper, for they are long and round and generally cigar-shaped. For such large fishes, they have extremely small mouths, and this is enough of a hint to conclude that they eat small particles of food. Frozen brine shrimp is greedily taken, though newly hatched brine shrimp is also a valuable addition to their diet. These fishes are excellent jumpers, so keep their aquarium covered at all times.

No one has yet been able to induce the Anostomids to spawn in the home aquarium, but many aquarists have seen them perform their strange nuptial dance. Sexes are practically indistinguishable.

The African Tetras

Most but not all Tetras come from South America. In the Congo River area of Africa are to be found some very beautiful, tiny Tetras. The genus *Neolebias* contains several small fishes which are peaceful and make valuable additions to the

community aquarium. They are available from time to time as tank-raised specimens, but they are difficult to spawn and are definitely out-of-range for the beginning breeder. Though the African Tetras are not as colorful as the South American Tetras, they do have interesting habits and most of them have large scales which reflect light so beautifully that they go well in large aquaria which contain many other fishes.

Arnoldichthys spilopterus, for example, has very large scales and enchanting red eyes. Red eyes are characteristic of many of the plain silver Tetras from Africa.

Combine the large scales with large eyes, and then add a tail which has a few rays extending from the middle, and you have two of the Congo Tetras, *Phenacogrammus interruptus* and *Alestopetersius caudalus.* These beauties, from the Stanley Pool, have been found to spawn in almost complete darkness. Their

eggs are scattered haphazardly into plant thickets, and too much light has been known to kill the eggs! At the present time, most of the African Tetras have been imported and there has been little commercial breeding success with them.

Larger Tetras

But odd breeding habits are not the sole property of African Tetras. Whereas *Pseudocorynopoma doriae* from Brazil spawns in a typical Tetra fashion by dropping slightly adhesive eggs in a haphazard fashion, with fertilization taking place as the male sprays sperm at the female while they knock against each other, *Corynopoma riisei* actually bats sperm packets at the female with his paddle-like pectoral fins. These sperm packets are aimed at her genital pore, and this is the only known Tetra that practices internal fertilization, though a few others such as *Glandulocauda* also of

+ *The sexes of the Swordtail Characin (Corynopoma riisei) are easily distinguished. The male has several of its fins elongate and modified for spawning. Some of these modifications are visible in this photo. Photo: H.-J. Richter.*

The male Sailfin Tetra (Crenuchus spilurus) is larger and more colorful than the female. This male can also be seen to have a relatively large mouth with sharp teeth, indicating it's not for the community tank. Photo: H.-J. Richter.

Brazil, and *Mimigoniates*, are suspected of a similar breeding technique.

Whereas most Tetras look alike in both sexes, some like *Crenuchus spilurus* are quite different. The male *Crenuchus* has large dorsal and anal fins, whereas the female's are short and less than half the length of the male's.

Astyanax bimaculatus is one of the few Tetras which is found over a huge range from the very tip of Trinidad and Venezuela, throughout Brazil to the tip of Southern Argentina. It is found both in warm and in cold water. Yet there are some other Tetras, like the Blind Cave Tetra from Mexico, that are found only in one small pool and nowhere else.

Just why the Blind Cave Tetra is blind is not known, but probably because it had been trapped in a cave many hundreds of thousands of years ago, and because it had no use for its eyes in the darkness, the eyes degenerated into mere useless pockets. But this doesn't stop the Blind Cave Tetra from breeding, finding food and swimming ceaselessly and effortlessly around rocks, plants and other obstacles. Perhaps the fish is guided by sound waves? Whatever sensory deprivation the Blind Cave Tetra has suffered, the fish is definitely able to compete for food with the other fishes in the same aquarium.

The Tetras are not all small fishes by any means. Many of them grow to four inches and larger, while some, like *Chalceus macrolepidotus*, may reach 12 inches in length. Then too, not all Tetras are community fishes, as they all have teeth and some of them use their teeth on their aquarium mates. *Creagrutus beni* and *Ctenobrycon spilurus* are two of these. While a perfect tank mate for a Cichlid, they should not be kept with other small Tetras. The same is true of *Prochilodus,* for while the teeth of the *Prochilodus* are small and used mainly for scratching algae from rocks, the fish are fast and can catch any fish small enough to be swallowed whole. But there are small Tetras, too, with large teeth and one of them, *Phago maculatus*, has teeth so sharp that it is able to attack a larger fish and actually chew him into bite-sized chunks!

While most Tetras swim in the middle strata of the aquarium, there are some species which inhabit the bottom (they are poor aquarium specimens, so none is illustrated in this book) and some stay at the top. Normally, top-swimming fishes eat insects. The Hatchetfishes from South America are insect-eating Tetras which are the only fish which can truly be called "Flyingfishes." While many fishes jump and spread their fins so they may glide, the Hatchetfishes of the genera *Carnegiella* and *Gasteropelecus* actually move their fins to help them fly! For the

aquarist there are Marble Hatchetfish and Silver Hatchetfish. Both color varieties are found in the two genera, and all need the same care. Hatchetfishes are peaceful and very interesting community aquarium fishes, but they do require some live foods which they can eat from the surface of the water. Small flies, such as the wingless fruit fly *Drosophila*, are excellent foods for these fishes. Keep their aquarium well heated and completely covered at all times.

Thus far we have examined slender elongated Tetras. Now we come to the round Tetras, and here we find a very mixed group. From the popular Black Tetras of the genus *Gymnocorymbus*, which are very simple to breed (they scatter eggs haphazardly into plant thickets) to the Piranha-imitators, the fishes of the genera *Colossoma* and *Metynnis*, which

+ The Black Tetra, Gymnocorymbus ternetzi, *is one of the most popular tetras around. As with most tetras, it is happiest when maintained in schools. Photo: Dr. Herbert R. Axelrod.*

eat mainly vegetable diets, we complete our categorization of Tetras by shapes.

The Piranha, one of the most ferocious of all fishes, has an interesting background story. It all started when President Theodore Roosevelt visited Brazil and witnessed a staged slaughter of a cow by a school of Piranhas. among 18-inch Piranhas and has never suffered a scratch. Though it is true that under certain circumstances, when they are crowded into a small pool due to receding waters and excited by the smell of blood and are starving, Piranhas are dangerous, but they do not normally travel in schools and few people are

! *Colossoma sp. cf.* oculus. *Pacus are good aquarium inhabitants when small, but they soon outgrow most aquaria. Vegetable matter is a necessity in their diet. Photo: A. Norman.*

He accurately reported that the Piranhas had stripped all the flesh from a mature cow in a matter of minutes. This is true! But it doesn't often happen that way in nature. The hosts of the President had herded the Piranhas into a small pool, and then they threw into this excited milling school a bleeding cow! You could do the same thing with a pack of French Poodles.

No one who has had experience with South American fishes is very frightened of Piranhas. The author often swims fearful of them during the normal course of swimming and fishing.

At the present time it is illegal to import Piranhas to the U.S.A., but some commercial breeders are spawning them and producing tank-raised specimens. They do require live foods, such as Goldfish or Guppies, from time to time, but many greedily take frozen brine shrimp too. Piranhas should not be kept with other fishes. As a matter of prudence, in the home aquarium Piranhas should be kept isolated, for if they are without food for a few days they will attack their own brothers.

In the world famous Shedd Aquarium in Chicago, a large school of Piranhas is displayed in an aquarium. This is a demonstration of very good aquarium management. The fish are well fed. The tank is furnished with caves and rocks which permit a chased fish to hide. The school consists of all sizes and this permits a pecking order to become established, much like what happens in a barnyard with a flock of chickens. The aquarium is large, several hundred gallons, and the fish establish their own private territories. Do all this and you too can keep a school of Piranhas.

Though big fishes should not, as a rule, be kept with smaller fishes, there are some large Tetras which make suitable tankmates for other small Tetras. *Leporinus* is a genus of very interesting cigar-shaped Tetras. They all grow large *(Leporinus fasciatus* grows to 18 inches long) but their mouths are so small that their diet is usually restricted to vegetarian foods. *Laemolyta taeniatus,* which grows to nine inches, is another peaceful fish suitable for the community aquarium. In order to protect themselves from cannibalistic fishes, *Leporinus* and *Laemolyta* are very "jumpy" fishes, and their aquarium must be covered at all times.

Two other very popular aquarium fishes which grow fairly large (an aquarium fish over five inches is considered *large),* but whose mouths are so small as to be considered harmless to community aquarium fishes, are the Headstanders, *Abramites microcephalus* and *Chilodus punctatus.* These fishes are always available in petshops handling the usual aquarium fishes and they are highly recommended for the community tank. They earned their popular name, Headstander, because they maintain themselves at a 45° angle while resting and swimming about in the aquarium. But like all peaceful, large fishes, they can

Some of the Tetra species would nibble on the plants in this combination coffee table/aquarium, but most of the Hyphessobrycon *species and the smaller Pencilfishes would be safe to leave with the plants—and they'd benefit from the shelter provided by them.*

jump several feet high without too much effort, so keep their aquarium covered at all times. Frozen brine shrimp is an excellent basic diet for all Tetras, large and small, ferocious and peaceful! Feed it to the Headstanders too.

While our Headstanders do just that, certain Hockeystick Fish stand on their tails! Actually *Hemiodus semitaeniatus* imitates this habit and doesn't spend much time in this attitude, but the *Thayeria* fishes, the real Hockeysticks (the English call them Penguins) always stay in the head-up position. There are several Hockeysticks, some more or less silver than others, but all are peaceful and make excellent additions to the community aquarium. They will eat regular dry food, but they prefer frozen brine shrimp and tubifex worms.

Glassfish and Nandids

A fish often mistaken for a Tetra is the Glassfish, *Chanda ranga*, even though this fish is an Asiatic species not at all closely related to the Tetras. Glassfish are found in hard, often brackish, waters, and they do not do well if kept in a community aquarium with fishes that like soft water without a heavy addition of salt. They must be kept by themselves to do well.

Another "oddball" is the Leaf Fish, *Monocirrhus*. This fish belongs to the family Nandidae which contains species in South America *(Monocirrhus and Polycentrus),* in Africa *(Polycentropsis and Afronandus)* and the *Nandus, Badis* and *Pristolepis* of Asia. All the South American and African species are carnivorous and capable of eating fish half their size.

Badis badis, also an Asian fish, is *not* a Cichlid but a Nandid. Its behavior is so typical of cichlid behavior that it is usually considered a Cichlid-type of fish. It requires live food; it is shy and retiring; and it changes colors so

+ The Indian Glassfish (Chanda ranga) *does better in a tank where some salt has been added. Although it has its own delicate beauty some imports have been "painted" with temporary neon dyes.*

The male Badis badis *is very secretive and requires hiding places in which to feel secure; a male* Badis *would soon find a retreat among the rocks in this planted aquarium.*

quickly that it has earned the name Dwarf Chameleon Fish! Interesting enough, even the spawning habits of *Badis* are similar to those of Cichlids with eggs being deposited on a leaf or in a "cave flowerpot" and carefully tended to by the parents. These fish are very sensitive to light, and too much of it will make them hide during the day.

The Cichlids

The Cichlids

The Cichlid group is one of the most interesting families of tropical fishes because it contains species which are intensely colored, along with interesting and unusual breeding habits. Beginning hobbyists are attracted to this group because many Cichlids can be induced to spawn in the home aquarium. Their major faults are their viciousness during the spawning ritual and their huge appetites. As a general rule, it is not safe to keep any fish of any species which is small enough to be ingested whole in with a Cichlid. Most Cichlids are hardy, and require a temperature that doesn't fall below 72°F. Cichlid aquaria should be large. A 20 gallon tank would be a minimum for the breeding of the larger species, while a five gallon tank would be sufficient for the smaller species. Although the majority of the Cichlids are carnivorous and require other fishes or worms as food, especially the beautiful and very popular Oscar (Astronotus ocellatus), there are some that enjoy large quantities of algae or young, tender shoots of aquatic plants. For these plant eaters the aquarist can still maintain an attractive aquarium today by using artificial aquarium plants for decoration. They are a miracle of fidelity and are absolutely non-toxic and non-fading. Then, to satisfy the fish, foods like Gordons formula with a high vegetable content may be used, and everybody will be happy.

There are even some species that eat "earth"! Geophagus cupido, from Brazil, gobbles huge mouthfuls of dirt, filters out certain edible parts, and spits out

! A Red Oscar. Astronotus ocellatus is a fish with a great deal of personality, and most who purchase one become quite attached to it, even though the species grows too large for any but the largest of home aquaria. Photo: A. Roth.

– *Fishes of the genus* Geophagus *are often known as "Earth–eaters" due to their habit of sifting through the gravel for anything edible. This attractive species is* G. surinamensis. *Photo: H.–J. Richter.*

the rest through his gills and the front of his mouth. Other Cichlids, like the Flag Cichlid, *Cichlasoma festivum,* eat anything they can digest. Both are popular as scavengers in an aquarium with large fish.

Regardless of the species you keep, live foods or fresh foods in the form of frozen brine shrimp, Tubifex worms, or even baby Guppies, are required by Cichlids in order to bring them into peak breeding condition. Incidentally, one drawback with live Tubifex worms is that they often bring disease organisms with them when fed to fishes. Fortunately, the aquarist may now obtain freeze-dried tubifex worms which contain all the nutrient values of the living product but need no refrigeration or running water for storage. The freeze-dried products have not been found to transmit any disease.

Larger Cichlids
The South American Cichlids of the genera *Astronotus,*

Cichlasoma, Aequidens, Pterophyllum and *Symphysodon* all have quite similar breeding habits. The male, usually the most colorful of the pair and with longer and more pointed dorsal and anal fins, selects an area on a flat surface where the female deposits her eggs after both fish have cleansed it thoroughly with their mouths.

While *Astronotus, Cichlasoma* and *Aequidens* species will be content to spawn on a flat rock, the more exotic species to be found in the genera *Pterophyllum* (The Angelfishes) and *Symphysodon* (The Discus-fishes) prefer a slanted or upright rigid flat surface, such as a large plant leaf or a piece of slate leaning against the side of the aquarium.

But with all generalizations there are exceptions, and one of the most highly recommended Cichlids for beginning aquarists, the Port, *Aequidens portalegrensis,* is such an exception. It never requires live

+ *The Firemouth,* Cichlasoma meeki, *is a truly gorgeous Central American cichlid. It is easy to breed and is not unduly aggressive. As in many* Cichlasoma *species, the male sports long dorsal and anal filaments that are an aid in sexing these fishes. Photo: H.–J. Richter.*

foods; its sex differences are very subtle with both male and female colored almost identically; it is peaceful and usually will not molest other fishes unless it is starved; and it will spawn on the bottom, on a slanted slate, or even on a piece of screening which separates the male from the female when they are in the same aquarium! Yet, with all the dangers of generalizing, it can be stated emphatically that Cichlids exhibit greater parental care of their eggs and fry than any other aquarium fishes.

All Cichlids lay their eggs with great care on a previously selected site. Then with most species the parents take turns in incubating the eggs. While this incubation process, with most Cichlids, is merely a fanning process to keep fresh water circulating over the developing embryos, some fishes actually take the eggs in their mouth (the Mouthbreeders), and suck water over them during their normal breathing operation.

The young are then herded and guarded against harm by both parents, and any intruder, regardless of size, is attacked with a ferocity quite out of proportion to the size of the fish. Spawning Cichlids will even attack the image of your finger against the glass of the aquarium.

The problems inherent in breeding Cichlids are quite easily overcome. First, you must have a pair — one male and one female. Usually this is easy. One standout exception is the Angel. It is virtually impossible for a novice to select a pair of Angelfish, *Pterophyllum* sp., with any degree of accuracy. Not only is the sexing problem difficult, but the differentiation between species requires a highly trained ichthyologist who can count the scale rows in a vertical line from the gill-plate to the middle of the caudal peduncle.

Pterophyllum scalare, the Common Angelfish, and *Pterophyllum altum* are so similar in appearance that color pattern alone cannot distinguish them. To complicate matters further, there is a third species, *Pterophyllum dumerilii,* which has also been occasionally imported. For all practical purposes, however, *Pterophyllum scalare* is THE Angelfish to be found in the aquarium.

The usual method of obtaining breeding stock is to buy a dozen baby Angelfish and raise them together in a 20-gallon aquarium. After a few months of good care and heavy feeding of live foods or meaty prepared foods, pairs of Angelfish will separate from the group preparatory to spawning. The breeder then isolates these two fish and usually ends up with a breeding pair. Unfortunately, two females sometimes spawn together, but the resultant infertile eggs are evidence of this unnatural occurrence.

Most professional breeders remove the eggs from the breeding aquarium and raise the fry in an aquarium without other fishes. The parents' incubation process is imitated very successfully by a fine spray of air bubbles, which carries a current of water over the eggs and the newly hatched fry. A small, inexpensive vibrator pump which draws less than five watts is quiet and reliable and can be bought in most petshops. Then, with a short length of air hose and a porous airstone, you have a 24-hours-a-day foster parent Angelfish.

So popular has the Angelfish been that many color varieties have been developed. These varieties occur as "sports"

Angelfish and Guppies are the two species maintained together in this nicely planted aquarium. Very few baby Guppies born in this tank would ever live longer than a few hours, as the Angelfish would seek them out and eat them as soon as they were born. Photo courtesy W. Paccagnella.

+ Cichlasoma festivum, *Flag Cichlid*

+ Cichlasoma nigrofasciatum, *Convict Cichlid*

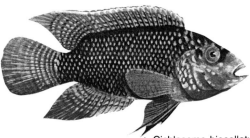

+ Cichlasoma biocellatum, *Jack Dempsey*

+ Cichlasoma facetum, *the Chanchito*

+ Aequidens pulcher, *Blue Acara*

+ Cichlasoma cyanoguttatum,
Texas Cichlid

− Crenichla saxatilis, *one of the*
Pike Cichlids

+ Uaru amphiacanthoides, *the*
Uaru

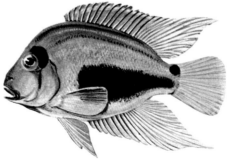

+ Dwarf Egyptian Mouthbrooder,
Pseudocrenilabrus
(Hemihaplochromis) multicolor

among the natural population. The most common variety is the Lace Angelfish. This is a darker-than-normal variety which first appeared in 1954. By successive inbreeding of these dark fish, a strain was developed which produces only Lace Angelfish. They are more delicate than normal Angelfish but are still hardy enough for the beginning aquarist to maintain successfully. They freely breed with normally colored Angelfish.

After selectively inbreeding darker and darker Lace Angelfish together, the first All-black Angelfish made its appearance. This was a major triumph for the professional breeder, but it was also a problem, for All-black Angelfish seemed to prefer breeding with normally colored fish, or at best, with Lace Angelfish. Pairs of All-black Angelfish breeding together successfully are very rare and the commercial breeders usually cross All-blacks with Lace Angelfish and are satisfied with 20% All-black offspring.

Breeders of Angelfish not only recognized black sports, they also were on the lookout for other color varieties and fish which had other abnormalities. Albino Angelfish have been found from time to time. Angelfish strains were developed where the front half of the fish was normally colored and the rear portion of the body was a solid black. This strain was named Half-black. But some Angelfish were noticed to have slightly longer fins than others, and by an intensive inbreeding program the famed Veiltail Angelfish were developed. Today, by careful crossing with All-blacks, Lace and Veiltails, Angelfish in any combination of these characteristics can be purchased at nearly every

Fishes to be put into an existing tank should be gradually acclimated to the temperature (and other qualities) of the water in the tank. Floating them in a plastic bag in the tank is one way to acclimate them, but they shouldn't be kept in the bag for too long.

petshop. The most rare is the All-black Veiltail Angelfish, but Lace Veiltails are almost commonplace. Perhaps, when you spawn Angelfish, you will notice a sport and thus begin a new strain yourself.

Of all the Cichlids, the Discus, *Symphysodon* species, is the most prized. This beautiful fish is extremely rare and very expensive. Only after thirty years of intensive research has there been any repeated successes in spawning this fish in captivity. Though it breeds exactly like an Angelfish, the baby Discus are parasitic on the parents and feed off the body slime which the breeding fish secrete at the proper time. Removal of the eggs from the breeding pair will only result in the death of the fry as soon as their egg sacs have been utilized as food by the developing embryos. Other species of *Symphysodon* have recently been made available, but all come from the Amazon River or its tributaries and all require copious feedings with like foods especially Tubifex worms , frozen brine shrimp and beef heart. Sex differences are extremely difficult to ascertain with any degree of accuracy.

Mouthbreeders are really a wonder of the aquarium world. Fishes of the genera *Tilapia* and *Haplochromis*, both from Africa (though *Tilapia* are now found all over the world) contain many species which incubate their eggs in the mouth of either the male or the female. With each species it is *either* parent that will carry the eggs. Parental care of the offspring does not end with oral incubation of the eggs, it goes much further than that. The parents tend their fry with intense devotion and protect them against any harm which threatens

+ A pair (male above) of Apistogramma reitzigi, *one of the Dwarf Cichlids*

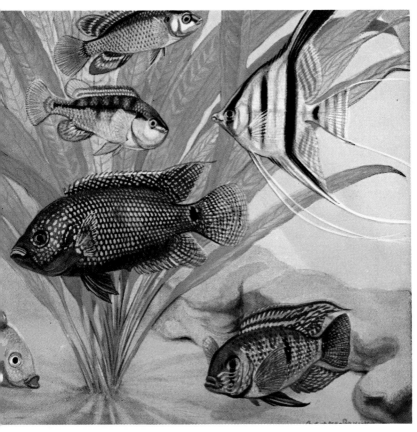

A tank housing the variety of different Cichlid species this tank does could soon become more of a battleground than a "community."

— Astronotus ocellatus, *the Oscar*

+ *This pair of Dwarf Egyptian Mouthbrooders,* Pseudocrenilabrus multi-color, *has just completed spawning. Note the expanded buccal pouch of the female, which is full of eggs. Photo: H.–J. Richter.*

their security. At the slightest approach of danger, the parent fish opens its mouth and the young swim in. So strong is this parental instinct that the parent incubating the eggs goes without eating for weeks, until his or her body has wasted away to about half of its original size...but the head remains large enough to accommodate the young ones. Some South American Cichlids of the genus *Geophagus* are also mouthbreeders, and there are also some among the air-breathers

Dwarf Cichlids
Dwarf Cichlids are miniature Cichlids which rarely grow larger than four inches. They are very popular because they can be kept in smaller aquaria and require

less care than their larger cousins. Unfortunately, most Dwarf Cichlids are shy and retiring, preferring to stay hidden behind rocks and plants. Even their spawning habits are inclined to be private affairs, quite in contrast to the larger Cichlids. The usual technique for breeding Dwarf Cichlids is to cut a hole in the side of a flowerpot and turn it upside down in the aquarium. The darkness and security offered by this cave make the Dwarf Cichlids feel right at home, and pairs spawn readily if properly conditioned on live foods or frozen brine shrimp.

Sex differences between Dwarf Cichlids are usually obvious. The males are much more colorful than the females. The fins of the males, too, are longer. In many species it is difficult to match males with females if several species are mixed, so similarly drab are the females.

The most popular of all the Dwarf Cichlids are the Rams, *Microgeophagus ramirezi*. They are very colorful fish, the female being the most colorful of all known Dwarf Cichlid females. For this reason, beginning aquarists are often confused when attempting to select a pair of young Rams, for there is no obvious color difference between the sexes. Quite in contrast is *Nannacara anomala,* where the male is gorgeously colored whereas the female is quite plain.

In nature, many species of Dwarf Cichlids are found in small streams which in Brazil are called *igarapes.* Dwarf Cichlids are not restricted to Brazil by any means, but are found in all the tropical countries of South America, from Brazil north to the Guianas and Venezuela.

Asia, too, is represented in the Cichlid group, and the Orange Chromide, *Etroplus maculatus,* is

+ *Female* Aequidens curviceps. *This is a peaceful, attractively colored dwarf Cichlid. The species is a substrate spawner and the parents are quite protective of the eggs and fry. Photo: H.–J. Richter.*

+ *Male (top) and female (bottom) of* Apistogramma steindachneri. *The males of most species of* Apistogramma *are brightly colored and nicely patterned, with extended, ornate finnage. Most are cavity spawners that prefer some sort of cave in which to place their eggs. Top photo: A. Norman; lower: K. Paysan.*

one of the rare Cichlids to be found in India and Ceylon. They, like *Microgeophagus ramirezi,* have sexes which are nearly equally colored, and this is one of the basic reasons for their popularity. They are more peaceful than the usual Cichlid.

+ Opposite Top: *Cockatoo Dwarf Cichlid* (Apistogramma cacatuoides). *Photo: H. Linke.* Opposite Middle: *Kribensis* (Pelvicachromis pulcher). *Photo: H. Linke.* Opposite Bottom: *Ram* (Microgeophagus ramirezi). *Photo: B. Kahl.*

Lake Malawi Cichlids — Mbuna

Africa is noted not only for its rain-forests and deserts, but also for its Great Lakes. At the source of the Nile River there are many lakes in what is known as the Great Rift Valley. The lake furthest to the south and of most interest to tropical fish hobbyists lies in what is now the country of Malawi, on the border with Tanzania and Mozambique, in an area once known as Nyasa. The lake is known as either Lake Malawi or Lake Nyasa, depending on whether you are reading new or old books. The waters of the lake are alkaline and the temperature is very constant, varying little from 26-27°C. (78-80°F.) Since there is little oxygen near the bottom of this deep lake, most fishes and invertebrate life are found near the shore and in the upper layers of the water. Lake Malawi has a surface area of over 11,000 square miles (more than that of the state of Maryland). It also contains almost 200 species of Cichlids, most found nowhere else.

Living near the shore are two genera of very prettily colored Cichlids known to hobbyists by the African name of **Mbuna** (pronounced EM-BOO-NA), and to scientists as *Pseudotropheus* and *Labeotropheus.* In recent years several species of Mbuna have been imported and bred, and these are now available to hobbyists in quantity and variety.

Before deciding to keep Mbuna, the beginner should realize that (1) the fish are expensive to purchase; (2) they require large tanks, preferably 50 gallons or more or they will be constantly fighting; (3) they require a great deal of effort in maintaining clean water and tank conditions; and (4) the fish are very sensitive to temperature changes. On the positive side are the unusual spawning behavior, the brilliant colors, and the very air of rarity and strangeness which these fishes possess. If you have been successful at keeping more common Cichlids and can afford the expense, then feel free to try the challenge of the Mbuna. Both *Pseudotropheus* and

— A fine specimen of the OB morph of Pseudotropheus zebra. *This is probably a male judging from the overall bluish cast seen in the spots on the body. Photo: Dr. H. Grier.*

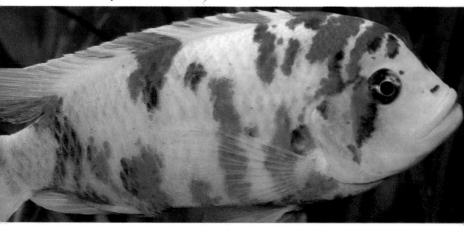

– A male "Marmalade Cat" Labeotropheus fuelleborni. *Normally, only the male of this morph has the black spots against a blue background. Photo: G. Meola.*

Labeotropheus are similar in many respects, both being adapted to nibble on thread algae growing on the rocky shores of the Lake. The mouth of Labeotropheus is definitely overshot by a projecting snout, forming an efficient tool for scraping algae; that of Pseudotropheus is more normal. In the aquarium, however, both Mbuna will eagerly accept many different types of living, freeze-dried and frozen foods, such as tubifex worms, blood worms, chopped earthworm, beef heart and liver, clams, and even flake food — these are certainly not picky fish!

Mbuna are very aggressive, especially between members of the same species. Although only 4 to 5 inches long, males are very territorial. They will claim a cave

– A female OB Labeotropheus fuelleborni, *with beautiful golden body color. Photo: G. Meola.*

or ledge as their own and vigorously defend it from all comers. If a specimen is added to an established tank—one in which every fish has found its place in the "pecking order" — there is a good chance that it will be killed or severely wounded by the other fish. The same is also true of females during spawning; a male might sometimes kill a female if she is not ready to spawn.

If there is enough room in the aquarium, Mbuna will also develop other habits sure to displease the aquarist. One of the favorite stunts is that of gravel moving. In this game the cichlids, especially males, build piles of gravel against the walls of the tank. This is probably done in an attempt to build shelters from prying human eyes and footsteps, so sometimes a dark strip along the bottom of the tank, starting at the level of the bottom, will give

the fish a feeling of security and they will not destroy your carefully laid bottom.

Labeotropheus is especially susceptible to fungus diseases and should be watched closely. An eye fungus is common, as is one on the gill covers. Diseased fish usually respond well to fungus cures to be found in the local petshop, but the safest approach is to prevent the spread of the mold. This is done by adding a small amount of salt to the aquarium water and by making sure that the temperature does not vary greatly from the usual 78-80°F.

Both genera of Mbuna are mouthbreeders, holding the eggs in the mouth until they hatch. Only females brood the eggs, but neither parent normally will try to eat the eggs or young. As the female approaches maturity, the colors of both sexes become much more brilliant and the males

— *Many mbuna species have blue males and yellow females. In* Pseudotropheus lombardoi *the case is reversed—the blue fish is a female, the yellow one a male. Photo: E. Isaacs.*

– Another of the many morphs of Pseudotropheus zebra. *This is the so–called "Cobalt Zebra," in which both sexes are solid blue in color. The color is usually more intense in the male, however. Photo: Dr. Herbert R. Axelrod.*

become more aggressive. Males begin to either dig a shallow depression in the bottom or to completely clean the surface of a flat rock. If other males or members of another species approach, they are driven off. Males may even practice a bit of mouth fighting like that of many other cichlids.

When a female Mbuna approaches, the male swims rapidly in her direction and then stops abruptly with a wave of the caudal fin. He then slowly swims toward the nest, trying to make the female follow. If she does not, he tries again. It is at this point that the female could be seriously mauled if she will not accept the male. Next the fish begin to chase each other's tails and then alternately take up what is described as a "T-position": one fish arches the body and begins to quiver while the other touches

the genital region. After a few such movements, actual egg laying begins.

At each effort the female lays three to six large yellow eggs which fall to the bottom. After picking up the eggs with her mouth, she then touches the male's genital area. By now the male has shed his milt, so sperm enters the female's mouth and fertilizes the eggs. This process is repeated until the female has laid all her eggs, usually about 40 depending on the size and age of the female.

The anal fins of both sexes are patterned with large yellow spots called "egg dummies." Some scientists speculate that these spots help ensure fertilization by mimicking eggs. In her effort to gather all the eggs she has laid, the female also tries to swallow the yellow spots on the male's fin. In so doing, she

- Above: *The Golden Peacock Cichlid* (Aulonocara nyassae *var.*) *is easily spawned and is in good supply.* Photo: R. Stawikowski. Below: *One of the variations of the peacock cichlids, the Yellow Band Powder Blue Peacock* (Aulonocara nyassae *var.*). *Photo: Schaller.*

engulfs a large amount of sperm near the male genital opening. This theory has never been proved or disproved, but it is an interesting look into why some fish have certain colors and others do not.

Females brooding eggs can be recognized by the swollen appearance of the back part of the throat. Little or no food is eaten for the 23 to 30 days during which the eggs are incubated. As soon as they absorb the yolk sac, the fry leave the mother's mouth, but they reenter when threatened at night. After about ten days the fry are on their own. The fry are relatively large and will eat newly hatched brine shrimp as soon as they leave the mother's mouth for the first time. In about one year they will be mature.

Among the Mbuna there are quite a few species, but not all are imported. Perhaps the most popular species is *Melanochromis auratus*, in which the males have a very dark blue-gray background color with two blue-edged yellow stripes. Females are much lighter. *Pseudotropheus zebra* is a blue fish with dark vertical stripes. In both species (and in the other species as well) there are also speckled and mottled phases, usually of dark on a light background. In these fishes sexes often cannot be identified until just before spawning since there are so many variable color patterns.

The two species of *Labeotropheus* are similar, being blue with darker stripes in both sexes. Both species, however, also have speckled females. *L. trewavasae* is more elongated than *L. fuelleborni* and usually has a reddish dorsal fin in the males.

Closely related to *Pseudotropheus* and *Labeotropheus* are species of the genera *Gephyrochromis*, *Cyathochromis*, *Petrotilapia*, *Genyochromis*, *Cynotilapia* and *Labidochromis*. There are many beautiful African cichlids yet to be seen.

— The morph of Aulonocara nyassae *seen most frequently has orange ventral fins and develops a rusty shoulder patch when mature. Photo: A. Norman.*

The Air-Breathers

While it is extremely rare for small oceanic fishes to be dependent upon atmospheric oxygen to breathe, it is not rare among the small freshwater tropical fishes. A large group of aquarium fishes, known to aquarists as "Labyrinth fishes" because of the labyrinth in the head which utilizes the oxygen contained in the air, have gained widespread favor among the hobbyists. These fishes are popular because they are usually very colorful, easy to breed, and easy to maintain.

Bettas

The best known of all Labyrinth fishes is the famed Siamese Fighting Fish, *Betta splendens*. It is true that many years ago, in Siam, small fishes were bred for their fighting ability. One of these fishes was the *Betta,* though it was not, by any means, the only fish utilized for fighting purposes. By intensive inbreeding and aquarium cultivation, beautiful color varieties of the *Betta* have been developed until they rival the beauty of the most gaudily colored Swordtails. These are solid reds, blues, greens and flesh-colored Cambodias. Albinos have appeared, but very irregularly and there is no established strain of albino *Betta* presently available. The mystery color is the all-black *Betta* and these have appeared in very dark chocolate browns and purple-blues, but thus far a Betta as black as a Black Molly doesn't exist.

One of the most fascinating aspects of keeping *Bettas* is to spawn them, for they are interesting breeders. Inasmuch as males must always be kept apart from one another (special Betta Display Tanks with small compartments are available at every petshop), females are usually maintained in the community aquarium with the other fishes. If your home is warm enough, you can keep your Bettas in small jars or brandy glasses spread throughout your home as living flowers.

When you want to breed them, merely introduce a female into a

+ *In a ripe female Betta, the abdomen is extremely distended with eggs, and the fish may bear some resemblance to one afflicted by "dropsy," which produces a similar swelling. Photo: H.–J. Richter.*

+ *Like many anabantoids,* Betta splendens *spawns beneath a bubblenest constructed by the male. Fine plants such as* Riccia *are good for helping to contain such a nest. Photo: H.–J. Richter.*

small aquarium of about three to five gallons capacity. The tank should be bare of gravel and plants except for a small bunch of *Anacharis* behind which the female may hide should the male become too insistent.

After the female has become established in the aquarium for a few days, the male can be introduced. He will take notice of the female almost immediately, but his attentions will be anything but amorous! Usually he will attack her ferociously, but this will rarely injure the female. Many hobbyists call this a pre-spawning test to be sure that the female is strong enough to breed. At any rate, if all goes well during these first few hours, the female will develop a tiny ovipositor, or egg tube, which will be noticeable as a small white tip projecting from her genital pore in the area of her anal opening. This white tip is a sign of a female's ability to spawn at that time. Older females, not in

the same aquarium with males, also develop this breeding tube, and these are the females to be selected for spawning.

Once the male's introductory activities are completed, he will start building his bubblenest. This he does at the surface of the water in a corner of the aquarium. By gulping mouthfuls of air and forming the air into mucous bubbles which he spits into a mass, a large nest is constructed. This nest can measure one inch thick and is six to eight inches in diameter. Upon its completion, the male dances with outspread fins before the waiting female and soon she will follow him under the nest where he wraps his body about hers and squeezes out some 20 or 30 eggs. As the eggs gently fall toward the bottom of the aquarium the male catches them in his mouth and spits them into his bubblenest. During this time the female floats motionless in the water as though paralyzed.

+ *In many anabantoids a spawning "embrace" takes place, with the male wrapping tightly around the female. Photo: H.–J. Richter.*

– One of the most sought–after Betta *species is the Brunei Beauty,* B. ma-crostoma. *This large species is a mouthbrooder. Photo: Dr. Herbert R. Axelrod.*

Should she revive before the male has all the eggs, she will usually eat them. The reason for a bare aquarium is now obvious...white eggs can be very difficult for the male to find if they fall between the crevices of white gravel! The male tends the developing fry during the first few days and he should be removed as soon as the fry are free-swimming. The female should be removed immediately after spawning...as she is liable to attack from the male.

Other Bettas also exist and they have similar breeding habits. *Betta bellica* breeds almost identically as *Betta splendens,* though the male is not as pugnacious. Also, whereas *Betta splendens* is an active alert fish, *Betta bellica* hides at the bottom and is hardly ever seen. *Betta brederi* breeds quite differently from both of the above; the male is a mouthbreeder and carries the eggs and young in his mouth until they grow too large to fit.

The Bettas come from the Thailand, Java, Borneo, and the Malaya area, and with them we find other interesting Anabantids. *Trichopsis vittatus,* which looks quite a bit like a wild *Betta,* is a very peaceful fish and the males get along fairly well together. It is often called the Croaking Gourami because it makes a noise when it gasps for air at the surface of the water.

Gouramis

But the real jewels of the Anabantid world are the larger fishes which aquarists call "Gouramis." The word "Gourami" is supposedly an Indian word as many of the airbreathing fishes come from India and Ceylon. The most popular of all Gouramis is the smallest, *Colisa lalia,* often called the Dwarf Gourami. It rarely grows larger than two inches... small when compared to the Giant Gourami, *Osphronemus goramy* (from which the name

Gouramis

"Gourami" comes) which grows to two feet in length and is considered as a good food fish. Some authors, mistakenly, call *Colisa fasciata* the "Giant Gourami" but the usual popular name for this species is the Striped Gourami. This is not a popular species because the males have their color only during the breeding season.

Whereas most other Anabantids in the genera *Betta*, *Belontia*, *Helostoma*, *Trichogaster* and *Sphaerichthys* do not put on elaborate spawning colors and males and females look very much alike, the fishes of the genus *Colisa* are completely different.

All Anabantids require live foods to bring them into condition. Their normal diet in nature is insects and insect larvae. In the aquarium, they do well on brine shrimp and tubifex worms.

One of the paradoxes in the aquarium world is the fish known as the "Kissing Gourami." Coming from Southeast Asia, this fish grows in nature to about 12 inches in length. Though the usual aquarium variety is a pink color, the wild specimens, known under the scientific name of *Helostoma temmincki*, are greenish. Why this colorless fish is so popular can hardly be attributed to its personality, for while the fish is rarely aggressive, it is difficult to breed, and requires special feeding to keep it full and rounded. Perhaps its great attraction lies in the name "Kissing" Gourami? This is the only fish which regularly puckers its lips when it meets another Kissing Gourami head on, and the two will lock lips in what appears to be a very amorous kiss. They will gently rock back and forth, lips locked and suddenly, after almost a minute of such affection,

+There are few freshwater fishes (or marine ones, for that matter!) to rival the colors of a breeding male Dwarf Gourami, *Colisa lalia*. In addition, the Gouramis of the genus *Colisa* are peaceful fishes suitable for any community tank.

+ *Colisa fasciata* is often referred to as the "Giant Gourami," though this common name is more properly applied to Osphronemus goramy. *Photo: Dr. S. Frank.*

smartly break away. Animal behaviorists are at a loss to prove the reason behind this strange behavior, for it has nothing to do with reproduction, mating, fighting or "cleaning each other's teeth"! Some authorities, without valid evidence to verify it, suggest that this is a threatening action similar to the ruffling of a bird's feathers, for the Kissing Gourami has been known, on very rare occasions, to attempt to "kiss" fish of other species. A truly magnificent sight is to watch an aquarium with a few dozen small Kissing Gouramis; when one starts "kissing" usually a few others will follow suit and the comical sight is enough to cause the most staid people to burst into laughter!

As aquarium inhabitants, only the small Kissers are of real value as the larger fish uproot plants and chase smaller fishes all about the tank. Though not nasty in the sense that they will eat or bite other specimens, when underfed they often "worry" a fish to death by chasing it continually, not allowing it to eat and giving it no time to rest. It must be advised that Kissing Gouramis be maintained in large aquariums, not smaller than 10 gallons, and that they be fed tubifex worms, frozen brine shrimp and, if available, salmon eggs (dried) or salmon egg meal. If not properly fed, this fish will certainly die of starvation, first going through a "hollow belly" stage that makes the fish look truly pathetic. Though not a fish for beginners, it is sold by the millions each year to the very people who haven't a chance of keeping it alive for more than six months. If you want Kissers, keep them alone in a tank of their own.

Standing alone with

+ *The Gold Gourami is a tank–bred strain of the Blue Gourami,* Tricho-gaster trichopterus. *Photo: H.–J. Richter.*

characteristics which are almost unique in the large family of the Anabantids is the legendary Chocolate Gourami, *Sphaerichthys osphromenoides.* Coming from Malaya, this fish has rarely been spawned in an aquarium. There are reports in the literature where widely scattered breeding episodes have been witnessed, but only one person saw them spawn at a time..and each has a very different report! Some people say they spawn like ordinary species which incubate their eggs in the mouth of either the male or female. Many Chocolate Gouramis captured in Malaya have been known to spit out their fry once they are placed in the collecting can after having been netted, but again, no proof. While other Gouramis are very hardy, the Chocolate Gourami is very delicate and difficult to keep alive. They must have live foods and relatively high temperature of about 85°F. and thrice daily feedings of brine shrimp, tubifex worms and some dry foods. Though sexes are very difficult to distinguish, males do have more intensely colored fins and have red edging on their anals. They are best maintained in an aquarium of their own, ideally five or six Chocolate Gouramis in a five gallon, heavily planted aquarium.

Going from the small Chocolate Gourami with its delicate characteristics to the *Trichogaster* genus with hardy, large, easily bred fishes makes one understand why the air-breathers are so popular. From the old favorite Blue Gourami (also called the Three-spot) which is the least expensive of all the Gouramis, to the angelic Pearl or Mosaic Gourami, these fishes are ideally suited to the beginning aquarist. A pair of Blue Gouramis, though difficult to sex (the female is fuller and the males have longer fins), is almost certain to spawn if they are kept alone in an aquarium and fed heavily on frozen brine shrimp for a few weeks. They all have huge bubblenests and lay up to 3,000 eggs at one time. They can be highly recommended as a first fish for a beginner.

As with all air-breathing fishes, they come up to the surface and gulp air from time to time. Some experiments have shown that unless the air-breathers are allowed to the surface, they will suffocate — other experiments show that not to be the case. Take your choice. The reason that these fishes have evolved this dual system of breathing is that they normally inhabit very warm pools with decaying vegetation which robs the water of dissolved oxygen.

The fishes of the genus *Trichogaster* include the Snakeskin Gourami, *Trichogaster pectoralis,* whose skin is supposed to resemble a snakeskin, and a beautiful, though rare, Gourami with pale blue color unmarked and unmottled which is called the   Moonlight Gourami.

Other Air-Breathers

In addition to the *Trichogaster* fishes which are peaceful, hardy and suitable for the community aquarium, and are called Gouramis, there are some air-breathers that come from colder water in China and Korea. These are vicious and not really suitable for the small community aquarium, and they are not called Gouramis. How the fishes of the genus *Macropodus* ever earned the name "Paradise Fish" will probably never be known. They have very interesting breeding

+ *Probably the most stately of the Gouramis is the Pearl Gourami,* Trichogaster leeri. *The male has the brilliant orange throat and lacy extensions to the anal fin. Photo: B. Kahl.*

Male Betta splendens, *Cambodia color variety*

Male Betta splendens

Female Betta splendens

Male Betta splendens

A community of labyrinth fishes: a pair of Pearl Gouramis, upper left; Thick-lipped Gourami male, bottom left; male Siamese Fighting Fish, bottom center; male Paradise Fish, top right; male Three-Spot Gourami, right center; pair of Dwarf Gouramis, bottom right.

habits, but no more interesting than the other Anabantids. Historically they were the first "tropical" fishes to be kept in aquaria, for they are extremely hardy and can do well in a small glass container without the aid of a heater. In the most strict sense of the word they are not *tropical* fish at all, but they are *aquarium* fish.

Not unlike the Paradise Fish is the Comb-tail, *Belontia signata*. It too is vicious unless kept with larger fishes, and it should be fed generously with live foods to keep it from bullying other fishes. About the only fish which can hold its own with this aggressive species is the Climbing Perch, *Anabas testudineus*. Though it grows too large for the usual home aquarium, it does make an interesting specimen when small. The Climbing Perch is able to walk on damp grass in very wet and humid areas. It is reputed to crawl in search of water as pools dry out in southern Asia.

The Rasboras and Danios

The Rasboras and Danios

From the giants of the aquarium world which breathe air from the surface of the water, we come to the midgets of the aquarium world which rarely come to the surface of the water except to snap at a floating piece of food. The Rasboras are small, colorful fishes from the tropical Indo-Australian archipelago, Southeast Asia and adjacent off shore island groups. The most popular is *Rasbora heteromorpha*. Though called by many popular names such as Harlequin Fish, Red Rasbora and Rasbora Het, it would be safe to walk into any petshop and ask: "Have you any Rasboras?" The proprietor would assume you mean *Rasbora heteromorpha*. So beautiful is this fish when in breeding condition that it far surpasses those displayed in most petshop aquariums. While Rasboras are very hardy, all species do not have the same requirements. *Rasbora heteromorpha* needs high temperatures, in the 80's, and ample feedings of live food or frozen brine shrimp. Without this care, they lose their beautiful coloring and become plain, pale and listless. In proper condition they are one of the most dignified beauties known to the aquarium world.

Both sexes in all Rasbora fishes look alike and it takes a real

+ *The Rasbora or Harlequin Fish* (Rasbora heteromorpha) *is one of the few rasboras almost always available to the average aquarist. A small group of them in a community tank without doubt enhances its beauty. Note the extent of the "lambchop" or "hatchet" pattern. Photo: H.-J. Richter.*

+ *The Espei Harlequin Fish* (Rasbora heteromorpha espei) *may at first be confused with the true Harlequin Fish, but when the "lambchop" designs are compared the difference can be seen.*

expert to be able to sex them. Too frequently an immature female is mistaken for a male, and the result is infertile eggs. Living in schools in nature, Rasboras can also be spawned in schools if some method is worked out whereby the non-spawning fish can be kept away from the eggs as they are laid. This is usually accomplished with a false base to the aquarium so the eggs can drop through the slotted bottom where they fall out of the reach of the other fish in the tank.

Caring for the scores of *Rasbora* species is very simple and because this group is so exceptionally suited for the community aquarium, they have earned a great deal of respect from commerical breeders, who find them fairly difficult to produce in commercial quantities. But for the aquarist this is no problem. A small (three to five gallon) aquarium is filled with crystal clear water with a pH of 6.4 to 6.8. The temperature

should be kept as close to 80°F. as possible and the tank should be planted with *Cryptocoryne* plants. Landscape the aquarium with foliage all along the back and sides and keep the center free for the *Rasbora* to school. Their behavior when with a dozen fish of the same species is quite different than when they are kept alone or in pairs. These fish do best when kept with their own kind. A small aquarium dedicated to one of the *Rasbora* species, especially *R. heteromorpha,* is well worth the effort.

The most tiny of all Rasboras is the Pygmy, *Rasbora maculata.* These are beautiful fish when kept by themselves and they lay eggs continuously if fed newly hatched brine shrimp, or even some frozen brine shrimp. The color of these fish in an ideal aquarium rivals even the regal beauty of *Rasbora heteromorpha,* but it is rare that people have the patience to maintain such tiny fish in a tiny aquarium where the

The iridescent gold stripe of Rasbora borapetensis *is particularly effective when a group of these fish are seen milling about in the midwater region of a tank. Photo: Dr. D. Terver, Nancy Aquarium, France.*

water must be maintained almost constantly at a pH of 6.4 with temperatures at least of 80°F. Soft water (water without an overabundance of dissolved salts in it) is another requirement.

While *Rasbora maculata* grows to one inch in length, *Rasbora trilineata, R. tornieri* and *R. taeniata* grow to three or four inches. The most simple of all Rasboras to breed is the Scissortail Rasbora, *Rasbora trilineata.* This fish reproduces very readily in the community aquarium and when a school of them are kept in their own tank, they deposit thousands of fertilized eggs into the plant thickets. Unfortunately the other Rasboras, though utilizing the same spawning process, are much more difficult to induce to breed.

In nature all of the Rasboras are to be found in small streams usually with clear, soft acid water, except *Rasbora meinkeni* of Sumatra and Java which seems to prefer pools. Though *Rasbora meinkeni* breeds readily, the females becoming so swollen with eggs that they look as if they will burst, the fry are difficult to raise and few of them attain maturity.

Although the identification of most fishes seems a fairly simple matter, there are many that pose philosophical problems as basic as "What is a true species?" One of these problem fishes is *Rasbora lateristriata.* The identification of fishes is based upon the comparison of certain physical characteristics which remain constant within certain groups. Human beings, for instance, with very little exception, have a backbone, two hands, ten fingers and toes, two feet, two eyes, a distinct number and kind of teeth, and range in size between 4 feet and 7 feet tall. Fishes are classified into similar categories, but what happens when the same fish is split into two populations and one grows for thousands of years in one part

+ *The Scissortail Rasbora,* Rasbora trilineata, *is not brightly colored but is the hardiest and most easily obtained Rasbora. Photo: B. Kahl.*

of the world and the other grows in a completely isolated area? Are these two distinct species, or is one a sub-species of the other? The population of *Rasbora lateristriata* which comes from Thailand is called *Rasbora lateristriata lateristriata* while the population which comes from the Malayan area is called *Rasbora lateristriata elegans.* Thus, a sub-species can be different from the parent species, or even identical to it, but, based upon the isolation of the two populations, differences do evolve. These differences are due merely to chance variations in the chromosomes, the microscopic cellular particles that give people,

+ *The tiny but brilliant* Rasbora maculata *is one of the smallest Rasboras, reaching only an inch or so in length. Photo: H.–J. Richter.*

+ *Rasbora kalochroma.*

and other animals, continuity of color, shape and form.

For use by the average hobbyist, though, the simple names *Rasbora lateristriata* and *Rasbora elegans* are enough. But compare the descriptions of the two fishes. One has a tail which is only mildly furcated (the V in the tail), while the other, *Rasbora lateristriata* has a deeply forked tail. One of the fishes has a dark line without a spot in the middle of its body, while the other has no lateral stripe and has two distinct spots, one in the middle of the body. Yet, by counting the rays in the anal fin (both have 3 spines and 5 rays), the dorsal fin (both have 2 spines and 7 rays), as well as the other fins, and by checking the teeth and other physical characteristics, the scientist can come to but one conclusion: Even though both fish may look different, they are identical in too many other ways to be considered as different species.

One of the convenient tests of sub-species is to breed them.

Thus far no one has been able to do this, though theoretically it would be simple enough if the fish had enough commercial value to warrant a full scale attempt.

Though not raving beauties, these two *Rasboras* are excellent for the community aquarium as they are large enough to take care of themselves.

The Danios and the White Cloud Mountain Fish

That your aquarium can be an international collection is only one of its attractions. But a mixed group of fishes in one tank need not all be 'tropical' fishes, and it is quite possible, under controlled conditions, to mix tropical fishes with coldwater fishes, Goldfish included!

In the White Cloud Mountains near Canton, China, a young boy named Tan discovered a beautiful small fish darting among the rocks in a mountain stream fed by melting snows. It took him days to catch a few of these magnificent beauties which were less than

The Danios and the White Cloud Mountain Fish

two inches long and when he finally captured a few it was discovered that they were unknown to science. To honor this inquisitive lad, the fish was named *Tanichthys,* which means "Tan's fish."

Tan took the fish home and put them into a small jar. As the sun shone on the jar the water became warmer and warmer, and soon it was heated to about 85°F.

Tan not only discovered the fish, but he found that these White Cloud Mountain Minnows could live in water either close to freezing or as warm as 85°F! Since that time the White Cloud has been a real favorite among aquarists, for it has many, many other qualities which make it the *ideal* fish for the beginner.

Since the White Cloud does equally well in warm and cold

+ *In captivity, where the mating of fishes can be carefully controlled and directed, it is possible to produce new strains with colors and/or finnage much different than those of the wild fishes. This long–finned White Cloud Mountain Minnow* (Tanichthys albonubes) *is an example of a fish selectively bred to enhance finnage. Photo: H.–J. Richter*

+ *One of the easiest egglayers to breed is the Zebra Danio,* Brachydanio rerio. *As seen here, they are easy to sex when fully conditioned—the female is considerably more robust than the male. Photo: Dr. S. Frank.*

water, their aquarium doesn't require a heater. They are small fish, very peaceful and omnivorous, thus they can be kept in a three to five gallon aquarium in perfect safety and fed the usual dry, prepared tropical fish foods. Of course live foods or frozen brine shrimp should supplement their diet, but they are not as necessary for White Clouds as they are for other fishes. Even these reasons would be enough to make the White Cloud a popular fish, but this fish is undoubtedly the most simple fish to breed. Males and females can be kept together in a heavily planted aquarium. Fine-leaved plants, such as *Myriophyllum* or *Cabomba,* should line the two sides and back of the aquarium. The White Clouds, after a magnificent dance executed by the male with widespread fins, will dash into the plant thickets and lay almost invisible eggs among the thick vegetation. In two days you will find tiny slivers, almost transparent, clinging to the sides of the aquarium. If the parents are properly fed they will not cannibalize the young.

As the White Cloud fry grow, they take on the coloration of a Cardinal Tetra, with a neon-blue stripe and red markings so vivid that you can hardly believe they are White Cloud babies. Just as they start to grow, additional fry will appear as the White Clouds breed continuously, laying a few eggs every day. By feeding both parents and fry newly hatched brine shrimp once or twice a week, you will soon have an aquarium filled with White Clouds...it's that simple.

Another fish which is practically indistinguishable from the White Cloud Mountain

Minnow is *Aphyocypris pooni*. This fish has more yellow and more red than the White Cloud and is often called the "German White Cloud." It is more expensive than the normal White Cloud. This fish requires the same care as the White Cloud and it is doubtful that true strains of either fish exist in captivity since they have been interbred so frequently.

In the same family Cyprinidae with the White Clouds are the very active fishes of the genera *Danio* and *Brachydanio*. These fishes come from India and adjacent areas. They are all small, very lively and are at their best when in with a school of 20 to 30 individuals. Their mouths are directed upwards which indicates they are surface feeders. They have small whiskers which scientists call barbels. Usually these barbels are in two pairs at the corner of the mouth. The Danios are very inexpensive fishes because they are so simple to breed.

Commercial breeders profit from the fact that Zebra Danios lay non-adhesive eggs. They usually set up a large aquarium and cover the bottom with marbles. By adding three inches of water over the marbles, they are assured that as the Danios spawn, the eggs will fall between the marbles, preventing the breeders from eating the eggs. The reason the tank is so shallow is that were the water deeper, the parents would eat the eggs before they had a chance to reach the bottom. Danios are very fast, agile fish, difficult to catch in a small net, especially in a heavily planted aquarium. If you want to catch them it is best to keep their tank covered with an opaque cloth so the fishes can be quickly captured when they are temporarily blinded by a strong light when the cloth is lifted. Feeding the Danios is simple. They are as omnivorous as White Clouds. Though they prefer frozen brine shrimp and dry, floating foods such as are sold in every petshop, a few tubifex worms or *Daphnia* (also available at petshops) make excellent additions to their diets. Since they inhabit the upper reaches of the aquarium, it is almost necessary to have a few scavengers in their aquarium to eat the food which has fallen to the bottom. *Corydoras* catfish are superior for this sort of task.

Catfishes and Loaches

The bottom-dwelling catfishes get their name from the cat-like whiskers (barbels) which project from their lips. On some the barbels are longer than the fish!

Catfishes range in size from the tiniest *Corydoras* that measure from one to three inches, to huge freshwater catfishes of the Amazon and Thailand which can swallow a pig in one gulp! They are valuable in the aquarium because they usually eat the food which has been missed by the other fishes and has fallen to the bottom of the aquarium.

Corydoras

Though mostly nocturnal, Catfishes which have found favor in the aquarium world are usually active at all times, and some are even a bit colorful. The *Corydoras* from South America are the usual Catfish offered in petshops throughout the world. They have very small mouths and are continuously poking into the gravel searching for whatever bits of food are available. They are perfectly peaceful and get along well with all but tiny, newly hatched fry which they will devour if they come across them. Usually *Corydoras* do not chase living foods as other fishes do, but merely graze, seemingly eating anything in their path.

The *Corydoras* are very interesting breeders, for the female apparently accepts the male spermatophores in her mouth. She then places these packets of sperm on a site which ultimately will be the resting place for a few eggs. Interestingly enough, during the spawning act the female ends up with the eggs cradled in her ventral fins. She takes them to the pre-assigned spawning site and attaches them to the spermatophores she previously placed there. Some authorities doubt that the female utilizes oral manipulation of the genital papillae of the male in order to obtain sperm, but merely to arouse the male so he can fertilize the eggs during the spawning act. Very often a group of *Corydoras,* as many as seven or eight, will join in a community egg-laying orgy which results in

+ *A group of the recently discovered catfish* Corydoras adolfoi. *This attractive fish is still a rarity and much in demand by catfish fanciers. Note the characteristic orange shoulder spot. Photo: Dr. Herbert R. Axelrod.*

+ A spawning pair of Corydoras paleatus *in the "T–position" characteristic of the genus and some related callichthyids. Photo: H.–J. Richter.*

hundreds of eggs being plastered on the glass sides of the aquarium.

Other Catfishes

In contrast to the bottom-feeding *Corydoras,* there are sucker-mouthed Catfishes which are utilized in the aquarium for keeping the algal growth, which develops on plants and glass due to excessive light, down to a minimum. These fishes, the most popular of which belong to the genera *Otocinclus* and *Hypostomus,* are recognized by their mouths which are found under the head. They have thick lips which also serve as hold-fast organs. The diet of these fishes is

+ Suckermouth Catfishes such as Hypostomus plecostomus *are without peer as algae controllers in the aquarium. Photo: A. Norman.*

mostly vegetable and they do a remarkable job of keeping rocks and other aquarium ornaments free from organic growths. The Sucker-mouth Catfishes are much more difficult to spawn than the *Corydoras* species. No one has spawned *Hypostomus* repeatedly and all commercially available stocks are imported.

Not all Catfishes are small scavengers content to subsist on leftovers or debris like the *Corydoras* and Sucker-mouths. There are some which are nocturnal prowlers which will greedily track down and gobble anything small enough to go down in one gulp. These nocturnal marauders are easily recognized by their very long barbels which reach past the anal fin in most cases. The *Pimelodus* Catfishes have a pair of maxillary (upper) barbels and two pairs of smaller mandibular (lower) barbels. These are believed to be

tactile organs which aid the Catfish to seek food at night and to assist them in swimming in complete darkness.

In order to keep these nocturnal Catfishes in good condition they must have a hideaway in which they can retire during the daylight hours. A flowerpot laid on its side serves this purpose very well, though a cave made of flat stones will be more decorative. About the only way to tempt *Pimelodus* and *Pimelodella* from their hideaway during the day is to drop a large earthworm within their field of vision. They *might* quickly swim out, snatch the worm, and quickly return to their lair.

These fishes are not recommended for the beginner because they have voracious appetites, gorging themselves until their stomachs are distended. It is not uncommon for them to remain peacefully in an

+ *Mystus micracanthus.* Photo: A. Norman.

+ *The famous Upside–down Catfish,* Synodontis nigriventis.

aquarium for a few weeks, only to devour half the tank's inhabitants in one night. How often people "can't imagine where those Cardinal Tetras went?" They probably were a tidbit for a *Pimelodus!*

Pimelodus clarias grows to a foot in length and this growth can be extremely rapid if there is enough food available. *Pimelodella gracilis* grows to about half the size and is considerably more peaceful than *Pimelodus,* though neither are to be trusted with small fishes. They make excellent scavengers for tanks containing such large fishes as the Cichlids.

When netting or handling any of the nocturnal Catfishes which have long barbels, be very careful. Their fins usually contain a strong, sharp, barbed spine which can only be removed from your hand with minor surgery!

Even netting these fishes is a problem as their spiny fin rays pierce the net and hopelessly tangle the fish as he thrashes about to free himself. Imagine what happens when some Catfishes (not illustrated here), whose bodies are nearly completely covered with sharp, curved spines, get tangled in a fine nylon net!

As yet nothing is known about the spawning habits of these Catfishes, though in nature they dig holes in the soft, muddy banks of the river and deposit their eggs in these small caves. When the river lowers during the dry season these holes number thousands per 100 feet!

One of the largest Catfishes kept in the aquarium is *Sorubim lima.* This is an interesting fish because although it grows in nature to at least two feet in length, they can be dwarfed by keeping them in small tanks without too much food, but take care...their mouths open wide enough to gobble down a fish wide as they are!

Not all Catfishes are kept in aquaria solely because they are good scavengers! Some, like the Glass Catfish, *Kryptopterus bicirrhis,* are valuable as an aquarium oddity. It does not scavenge at all and requires rather delicate treatment to keep it alive. Live foods are a must, though frozen brine shrimp will sustain life. This is one of the few Catfish which rarely, if ever, feeds continuously from the bottom of the aquarium. It has to be very hungry before it will feed there! Offer the Glass Catfish Tubifex worms, and it will devour them until its small stomach almost bursts.

Other Catfish oddities are the Electric Catfish, from Africa, which can give off an electrical discharge strong enough to hurt a man and stun a small animal; the Upside-down Catfish schools by the millions every night in the Stanley Pool, Congo River...but it swims upside-down. Its protective coloration has adapted to this development and it has a dark belly and light back, just the opposite of most other fishes! *Microglanis parahybae,* a South American species, is kept as an ornamental fish because its coloration is so attractive. All Catfishes prefer a darkened aquarium and the best way to limit their days is to keep them in a well lit tank which has a light on it at night. Since an aquarium must have light for the plants to survive, it is recommended that plastic aquarium plants be utilized if you plan on keeping some of the Catfish oddities in an aquarium by themselves. Petshops very often classify all Catfishes as scavengers. *They are not!* Do not buy Glass Catfish or any Catfish with a large mouth and expect them to clean small uneaten food particles from the bottom.

Loaches

Not all scavengers are Catfish. There are some small fishes called "Loaches" which have eel-

+ *Microglanis poecilus is one of a number of very similar Bumblebee Catfishes. When small they are good community tank fish, but may eat small fish as they grow large enough to swallow them. Photo: H.–J. Richter.*

+ *Acanthophthalmus myersi.* Photo: B. Walker.

+ *Misgurnus fossilis.* Photo: R. Zukal.

like bodies and these make ideal scavengers. They are continuously poking about the roots of plants, eating the smallest particles of food and being so peaceful and unobtrusive that they are hardly ever noticed. Some dealers sell these Loaches as "Japanese Weather Fish." They are reputed to swim on the bottom when the weather is going to remain the same and swim on the top when there is a drastic change in weather about to take place. Unfortunately they rise from the bottom in large lakes because the lack of sunshine creates a high carbon dioxide content in the lower reaches of the lake and the Loaches swim where the water has a richer oxygen content, namely the water closest to the air!

Catfishes and Loaches are, as a general rule, very partial to soft water and the introduction of salt as a tonic may help the other fishes, especially the livebearers, but it may kill the Catfishes and Loaches. Don't add salt to an aquarium without insuring there are no Catfish in the tank.

The Barbs

The Barbs

A group of small, colorful, active fishes inhabiting the tropical waters of Asia and Africa, the Barbs are very popular aquarium fishes. Their common name has derived from the similarity of these fishes with the European Barbel *Barbus barbus,* which science has definitely shown to be unrelated. Though much more taxonomic work is needed on this group of fishes, only ancient aquarium books adhere to the scientific name of *Barbus* for the fishes in this genus. For the purpose of this guide, the generic name *Puntius* will be used, though certainly many of the Barbs illustrated here belong in other genera. Essentially the main generic difference between these Barbs is merely the number of whiskers (barbels) they possess; their care, breeding, feeding and aquarium needs are the same.

Small Barbs

In the aquarium the Barbs are the clowns. Always moving, chasing other fishes, poking among the debris and snapping at anything moving through the water, the Barbs present perpetual entertainment to the casual observer. An aquarium devoted exclusively to Barbs is recommended for displays which are maintained in such public places as restaurants, doctors' offices and the lobbies of buildings. They are not timid fishes and do not hide or shy away from strange shadows or the inevitable taps on the glass which demoralize many other aquarium fishes.

Being very active, their oxygen requirements are much higher than those of Catfish, Characins or Livebearers, and their aquarium should be equipped with aeration equipment and a heavy-duty filter. These are relatively inexpensive aquarium accessories and a 20 gallon aquarium can be outfitted with all the essentials at a reasonable cost. Barbs are also voracious eaters and they gorge themselves on dried foods. Care should be taken when feeding Barbs the ordinary tropical fish foods which come in small cans. If too much is

+ *Occasionally "sports" appear in breeders' stocks, and sometimes these mutants are fertile and breed true. A case in point is the Moss Green Tiger Barb, which does not exist in nature. Photo: H.–J. Richter.*

+ *Two males of the Rosy Barb,* Puntius conchonius. *Females are usually a duller greenish–bronze color. Photo: B. Kahl.*

offered at one time, the Barbs will eat it so quickly that it will not have had time to absorb its capacity of water and, as a result, their stomachs will become bloated. The increased pressure on their internal organs will temporarily cause an imbalance in their swim bladder. This results in the Barbs being unable to swim in a straight line, instead they do the "roller coaster" bobbing up and down, fighting to keep their balance. In a few hours they will have excreted most of the food, undigested or, at best, partially digested. These droppings will then tend to cloud the water as bacterial action will have been initiated in the lower intestine of the fish.

Pelletized tropical fish foods, fed sparingly, tend to minimize the danger of putrefying the aquarium. Never feed Barbs more than they can completely ingest in three minutes. Better, feed them two or three times a day, sparingly, rather than one heavy feeding per day. Of course, feedings with live foods such as Tubifex worms or *Daphnia,* or

with frozen foods, eliminate the possibility of the fishes eating material which doesn't contain sufficient water. Barbs are completely omnivorous fishes and eat anything that other fishes will eat. As a result their diets should contain some vegetable matter or they will surely attack the aquarium plants and reduce them to shreds. The larger Barbs, such as *Puntius filamentosus,* will probably attack the aquarium plants anyway and the only way to maintain a decorated aquarium is to use plastic plants or to place a glass partition between the fishes and the plants. This partition is invisible from the outside and can also be used to separate active, vicious fishes from smaller, timid species. The glass is secured to the sides of the aquarium with U-channel rubber and is held in place by a snug fit. The smaller Barbs are much less apt to munch on plant leaves and of all the species illustrated here only *Puntius filamentosus* is dangerous in this respect.

Many Barbs are difficult to sex when the breeders are not in proper condition. The most popular of all Barbs, the Tiger Barb, *Puntius tetrazona,* has both male and female colored alike and the only way to sex them is to look for a slender male with a red nose and lips. The female will have a silver nose and she should be distended with eggs. *Puntius dorsimaculatus* are colored alike, though for a very short time during spawning time the male has a reddish-purple tinge. The same is true of *Puntius dunckeri,* though the male will keep his intense reddish coloration for as long as he remains in breeding condition, which may be weeks or months. *Puntius conchonius,* on the other hand, is only a plain silver fish until the male becomes mature and if he is fed and maintained properly, he will have an intense reddish coloration. This breeding color fades at times to a rosy color (thus the popular name "Rosy Barb" for this species) but the female always remains a plain, silver fish.

It is quite common with most fishes and birds that the male of the species is more colorful and more adorned. Whereas most male birds are intensely colored and may have longer feathers, the same is true of many fishes and in nearly all instances where the sexes have different coloration and one of the two has longer fins, it will be the male that is endowed with the excess.

Animal behaviorists, those scientists whose interest lies in determining why animals react to various stimuli, have hypothesized that male birds are more colorful to distract potential enemies from their colorless mates which may be sitting on eggs. With fishes this theory is untenable, for the male and female Barbs both participate equally in reproduction and neither ever pays any further attention to their eggs once they have spawned (unless they eat them!) So, for the present, there is no logical explanation for why male Barbs are so highly pigmented during their breeding season, unless it is to attract females of the same species.

There is another interesting characteristic about Barbs. Consider for a moment the group of Tiger Barbs which includes *Puntius tetrazona, P. hexazona, P. pentazona* and *P. partipentazona.* These fishes are all colored alike, grow to the same size, are found in adjacent territories and are identical in most physical characteristics *except* they have a different number of stripes on their body. If you were able to

This artist's conception of a community aquarium houses fishes of seven different families and includes a few species whose requirements are at odds with those of the others in the tank.

compare these fishes with each other in an aquarium, it would take careful study to discern which was which! Yet, as similar as these fishes are physically, they have considerably different aquarium requirements. *Puntius hexazona* is a very meek, mild Barb that requires soft acid water and a feeding of frozen brine shrimp every day in order for it to stay alive. *Puntius tetrazona* needs no special care and gets along well on a minimum of attention as long as ample food is provided. *Puntius pentazona* is a very shy and retiring fish which doesn't school and prefers a dark, quiet aquarium, yet *Puntius partipentazona* is quite the opposite and stays in open water, schooling tightly with other Barbs and showing few, if any, retiring characteristics.

One popular aquarium fish, the Golden Barb, *Puntius schuberti,* is probably not a fish which exists in nature. A fish-breeder named Tom Schubert who was quite successful in the 1940-50's in New Jersey, 'discovered' a light colored Barb among his fishes. By constant inbreeding he fixed a golden yellow strain which he catalogued on his price list as "Barbus schuberti" but which to this date has never been found in Asia, the area from which this fish was credited.

Whereas there are many larger Barbs, such as the Spanner (Monkeywrench) Barbs, from southeast Asia, especially the Malayan Peninsula, which may grow to seven inches in length, there are some island Barbs which never attain a length greater than two inches, and even that is a rare, maximum size. Both Puntius nigrofasciatus, the Black Ruby Barb, and Puntius oligolepis, the Checkered Barb, are found in

As in many other barbs, the female of Puntius ticto *is larger, heavier, and less colorful than the male. Most barbs are not difficult to breed and scatter their eggs among fine–leaved plants. Photo: R. Zukal.*

+ The true identity of the Gold Barb is somewhat a mystery, as the fish does not appear in nature. Possibly it is a form of Puntius sachsi or P. semifasciolatus.

rather isolated areas on large islands. *Puntius nigrofasciatus,* probably the most beautiful of all Barbs when the male is in breeding color, is found in Ceylon in shallow, slow-moving pools, where they dash about eating small Crustacea and the luckless fry of other fishes which are swept into the pool. These Barbs, unless kept in perfect condition, with ample feedings of live foods and frozen brine shrimp, will never show the magnificent color for which they are famed. Yet, if just fed ordinary canned tropical fish foods, they can live for years, never reaching breeding condition and never wearing their gaudy breeding dress.

Puntius oligolepis, on the other hand, is found in Sumatra, and comes from shallow, fast-moving streams where they, too, feed upon vegetation, Crustacea and other small living creatures. Their coloration, regardless of their diet as long as it is ample, remains the same and during their breeding cycle, the male intensifies in coloration an almost unappreciable amount. This Checkered Barb is a good addition to a Barb tank, but to maintain them alone would be almost wasteful. When it comes to daily beauty and activity the fish with the most color is still *Puntius tetrazona.* Its breeding colors are almost the same as its normal dress. If you want spectacular color during certain seasons of the year try the Rosy Barb, *Puntius conchonius* and the Black Ruby, *Puntius nigrofasciatus.*

Another very popular species of small Barb is the Cherry Barb, *Puntius titteya.* The male, which is normally a brownish color, becomes a deep cherry red when ready to spawn. Females have a chocolate stripe on the sides which merely becomes a shade deeper at this time. This fish is easily induced to spawn, and the same may be said of *Puntius phutunio,* another dwarf species.

The Barbs are among the most easily bred of all aquarium fishes. Tank size required varies with the size of the species. The so-called "dwarf" species require only a five gallon aquarium. This would include such species as *P. gelius* and *P. cumingi.* The medium-sized Barbs, like *P. tetrazona,* are more easily spawned in 10 to 15 gallon aquaria, and the large Barbs require 20 gallons or more. Their aquarium should be planted heavily with an open space in the center front to give them swimming room. Some breeders prefer to use two males to one female, but as a rule it is better to use only one. If both fish are ready for spawning when placed in the breeding aquarium, a wild chase will begin almost at once, with the male doing all the pursuing. Soon the female will

+ *Cherry Barbs,* Puntius titteya, *spawning. Photo: H.-J. Richter.*

+ *A spawning pair of Tiger Barbs. The eggs are shed into the plants, where they adhere until hatching. Several color varieties of this species are available including an albino form. Photo: H.-J. Richter.*

come to a halt in a thicket and the male will take a position tightly alongside her. Both will quiver for a few seconds and about a dozen eggs are dropped among the plants. This act is repeated until the female is depleted, at which time both lose interest and if not removed at once will begin to hunt eggs and eat them. Eggs hatch in 48 to 72 hours for most species, and the fry need not be fed until their yolk-sac has disappeared, at which time they begin to hunt hungrily for food. As the Barbs are omnivorous feeders, providing them with food is no great problem. Most commercially prepared foods include a very fine grain, and because they are bottom-feeders it is best to stir their food into a tumblerful of water before feeding to make it sink to where the Barbs are looking for it. Growth is very

rapid, and a tankful of tiny Barbs always on the move and constantly searching for bits of food is an attractive and interesting sight. Newly hatched brine shrimp is the ideal food for *all* fry, Barbs included.

If we were to make a study of all the Barbs in the world (and the number would be an imposing one), we would be surprised to find that a great number of them come from Africa as well as Asia. Still, we see mostly Asian species for sale among the dealers. There are a number of reasons for this. In the first place, most of the African Barbs are not quite the beauties that the ones from Asia are. Even if they were (and a few of them definitely are!), most of them are more difficult to maintain and spawn. During one of his visits to the United States, Pierre Brichard, the well known

fish collector from Africa, spoke about some Barbs he had found in tiny backwater streams which were brilliantly beautiful. When he examined the water and tested it, he found that there was such a concentration of decaying vegetable substances that the water was highly acid, so much so that it seemed unbelievable to him that fish could thrive in it. Such water could be duplicated in the aquarium, but certainly no other types of fishes could be kept with them. If they were hardy, the aquarium hobbyist would certainly not let this difficulty stand in his way, but they were found to be very delicate as well. We are always learning new and better

Side by side, the freshwater and saltwater community aquariums shown here provide the room with a vista of living beauty. Photo courtesy of Werther Paccagnella.

techniques in fish-keeping, but a few species are still even too delicate to withstand the short trip from their native streams to the collector's compound, much less the longer journey to the dealers thousands of miles away who are anxious enough to distribute them. The poet's statement that "many a flower is born to blush unseen" could just

as well be applied to many African Barbs.

It is also true that a good many of the hardier African Barbs are a rather colorless lot. Of the three species *P. trispilos, P. unitaeniatus* and *P. werneri, P. unitaeniatus* has been spawned.

A Barb-like fish from Asia which is sometimes found in Thailand and Malaya, is the Bony-Lipped Barb, *Osteochilus vittatus.* Not a very suitable candidate for mixed company, it can only be kept with fishes large or larger than itself. Although specimens more than a few inches long are rare, the fish grows to nine inches in its native waters and it may easily outgrow its welcome in an aquarium where it was housed when small. This fish has a peculiar lip formation. The rough upper lip is shaped like a horseshoe and is bone hard; the softer lower lip fits inside. There have been only a few importations since this fish was first introduced in 1954, and so far there are no reports about their spawning. Perhaps the imported fish were too small to be sexually mature, or nobody was interested enough to make the attempt to get them to spawn. Once established in an aquarium which it finds to its liking, the Bony-Lipped Barb usually proves to be very hardy and lives for a long time without any special pampering. There is a very similar species, *Osteochilus hasselti,* which grows larger and does not have the dark stripe on its side. Both species are peaceful for their size, and their maintenance in home aquaria is no problem except that they may grow too large for their quarters. If they do, your petshop will probably exchange them for other fishes.

One of the most attractively colored of our fresh-water aquarium fishes, and certainly the most beautiful of the *Botia* genus, is the Clown Loach, *Botia macracanthus*. The hobby is still dependent on importations for these very attractive fish because they have so far resisted all efforts to spawn them. A tankful of these beauties, baby-sized, would be no problem at all for a dealer to dispose of. But here, as with so many others, we cannot even tell the boys from the girls. Perhaps the Asiatic breeders have solved the mystery, and are only sending us one sex? This is

one way to keep outsiders from learning the secret. Then again, there may be no secret and some day some fortunate soul who gives his fish a little extra care will be amply rewarded. Most of the *Botia* species are largely nocturnal, but this does not seem to be the case with the Clown Loach. They like to hide in shady spots at times, but do not seem to have any great aversion to light. Like the other Loaches, they are provided with barbels which proclaim that they are bottom feeders, as these barbels are tactile organs which help them to detect their food.

The Loaches have a unique way of protecting themselves. There is an erectible spine in front of each eye, which the fish causes to stand out when alarmed. Many a predatory bird or fish has choked to death when he tried to swallow one and could not get it dislodged.

+ *Labeo frenatus, like its relatives in the genus, is known in the pet trade as a "shark." This is unfortunate, as it gives the uninformed the impression that these are aggressive fishes, when in fact they are very peaceful. Photo: R. Zukal.*

+ *The Red–tailed Black Shark,* Labeo bicolor, *is usually grayish in color with a pink tail when young. As it matures, however, the body becomes velvety black and the tail bright scarlet, making it a very popular fish. Photo: B. Kahl.*

Sharks

There is nothing shark-like about the behavior of the Redtailed Black Shark; it merely got its popular name by the appearance of its dorsal fin. From the moment it was introduced this fish was an immediate hit, with its coal-black body and bright red tail. Males of this species select a part of the aquarium for their own occupancy and defend their "territories" against intrusion. They bluff fierceness with the hope that their bluff will not be called, because they have no real dental equipment for attack or defense. A great number of these fish have found their way into the American market in the last few years from Thailand, where they are being bred in outdoor pools. The amazing thing is that with so many fish distributed among American and European hobbyists, we still have very few accounts of their spawning, and as far as is known, few have been able to do it in the aquarium as yet. We will never know all there is to know about aquarium fishes, but we are always learning more. Mother Nature helps the breeders in the tropical countries. They merely dig a mud pool, introduce a few hundred fish, then wait for developments. Many species which have defied the most skilled efforts of experienced breeders are easily produced in this manner.

The Black Shark is also a "shark" in name only. A specimen about 10 inches long is an imposing sight; at this size they still have their coal-black coloration in the body as well as the fins but as they get older their color fades. The tail, especially, becomes lighter in color and rows of white dots appear on the sides. It is also amazing to see how they seem to fare quite well in an

+ *Many species of fishes are available in tank–bred albino forms. This is an albino* Labeo bicolor. *Photo: A.Norman.*

aquarium which seems to be much too small. They can be seen in an aquarium seemingly happy in a space where they scarcely had room enough to turn around.

It is not a good idea to keep a number of Black Sharks together, as this may lead to some pitched battles. This is also a fish which takes possession of a territory, and in an aquarium of average size, a large fish is liable to consider the entire tank as his personal property and constantly harass and chase any other fishes put in with him.

+ *The Rainbow Shark* (Labeo erythrurus) *is peaceful toward other fishes but if kept in cramped quarters will tend to quarrel among themselves. Photo: Braz Walker.*

– Labeo variegatus is one of the rarer "sharks" in the aquarium trade. The mottled juvenile (top) usually darkens as an adult (bottom). Photos: B. Walker.

It must be kept in mind that Black Sharks have a healthy appetite; they could even be accurately referred to as "greedy." If you want to keep them in tip-top condition, they must be given heavy feedings of frozen brine shrimp, supplemented by vegetables such as spinach or lettuce leaves. Lacking a sufficiency of these, the fish may never attain full size.

The Killifishes

The Killifishes, Including the "Annuals"

Call them Killifishes, Minnows, Toothed Carps, Cyprinodonts or whatever you like, the Killifishes are a fascinating group. They include some of the most colorful of all aquarium fishes, some with the most interesting living habits imaginable. There are many things which can be said in their favor as aquarium fishes, and a few which detract slightly. One detracting or distracting aspect of keeping aquarium Killifishes is that their scientific names are not all well established among aquarists, and even among ichthyologists. For example the Blue Gularis is well known to aquarists. It hasn't changed, nor has its "common" name. But in scientific literature it has been called *Fundulus gulare*, *Aphyosemion gulare*, *Aphyosemion caeruleum*, and most recently it develops that the first Blue Gularis was scientifically described and named *A. sjoestedti*. Unfortunately, there is another fish, the Peacock Fundulus, which has also been called *A. sjoestedti* for many years. The names are muddy, the fish are beautiful.

Although we present only one Killifish native to the United States in this guide (space does not permit more), there are many others found in our coastal waters, occurring in such numbers in places that they are used by fishermen for bait with which to catch larger fishes.

Aphyosemion

Our first Killifish is a very popular African species, the Lyretail, *Aphyosemion australe*. The fishes of the genus *Aphyosemion* spawn in two very different ways. There are the top-spawning species which lay their eggs in plants near the water's surface. These eggs hatch in just about two weeks. The youngsters have already absorbed their yolk-sac during the incubation period and are able to swim freely and take newly hatched brine shrimp at once. Most *Aphyosemion* species

— The normal color form of Aphyosemion australe. *There is a gold color form more common in the hobby. Photo: Dr. S. Frank.*

– The red–spotted male Aphyosemion chaytori *is a lovely fish. The female, like most other female killies, is very dull in color. Photo: V. Elek.*

are top-spawners.

The top-spawning *Aphyosemion* species prefer to remain in the upper reaches of the aquarium. They are very efficient hunters and their sharp eyes are always quick to detect the presence of any live food in their aquarium. They stalk their prey and with a motion that looks like drifting they approach and grasp it with a lightning-fast motion. This makes them dangerous to any fish small enough to be swallowed. Males are always easy to distinguish.

The male Aphyosemion occidentalis *is a pleasing and unusual burnt orange color. Photo: H.–J. Richter.*

— Many killifishes, such as the pair of Aphyosemion occidentalis *seen here, are plant spawners. Photo: H.–J. Richter.*

Mother Nature was exceptionally lavish with her colors where males were concerned, and much more conservative with the females. The males usually sport larger and gaudier fins.

Spawning does not take place in a few hours, as is the case with most fishes, but is a drawn-out proposition which can extend over several weeks and even months, a few eggs being laid

daily until such time as the female has become depleted. This presents a bit of a problem to the hobbyist who is trying to raise a large number of youngsters. Incubation, of course, begins when the eggs are laid and ends when the fish hatch. With eggs being laid every day, naturally they will hatch in the same order. The result is a batch of youngsters of mixed sizes, and eventually there is a very real danger of the younger, smaller ones being eaten by their older brethren. One way to protect them is to keep them sorted according to size until they are too big to be swallowed. Another method is to use a large, heavily planted aquarium and simply remove the larger youngsters as they begin to mature. Either way, growth is rapid, and the wait is not a long one.

The spawning is interesting. The male is a tireless driver and pursues the female all over the tank. Many aquarists use two females to one male to prevent injury to females. When the female is ready to expel her eggs, she comes to a stop among the plants. The male takes up a position beside her and they engage in a quivering embrace. When the egg is dropped the male catches it in his anal fin and fertilizes it, then flips it into the plants. Each egg hangs from a little thread like a ball from a Christmas tree branch.

It might be best for a beginner to remove the eggs every two days and hatch them separately. With a light behind them, they are easy to see and may be removed by picking off a bit of the plant to which they are attached with a pair of tweezers. The eggs are protected by a rather hard shell and may be removed gently with the fingers as well. A small shallow container suffices for the eggs until they hatch, and they can then be transferred to a "raising aquarium."

The fact that the eggs of the top-spawning *Aphyosemion* species take two weeks to hatch has led to an interesting phase of fish-keeping. There is ample time for a hobbyist to gather freshly-laid eggs from his fish, place them into a small bottle of water from their aquarium and mail them to a friend. The resulting exchange had made possible the keeping of many previously little-known species in places where they would otherwise be unknown. Toy plastic baby bottles are perfect egg shipping containers.

We now come to one of the oddest groups of fishes, the bottom-spawners or "annuals." These fishes have made a seemingly impossible adaptation. Their habitat is flooded for a good

— The coloration of Aphyosemion seymouri *is somewhat subdued but is offset by the nicely contrasting orange tail. Photo: H.–J. Richter.*

part of the year during the rainy season. Then, when the dry season comes along, the waters recede and the ponds where our fishes are found gradually contain less and less water. The fish population is crowded into always smaller quarters, and when the waters dry out completely the fish have become stranded and die. This would seem to be the end of the cycle, but when the rains come and the ponds fill up again, a new crop of fish appears as if by magic. The answer, of course, is that the eggs, which are laid in the mud bottom, can withstand a period of drying to tide them over the time when there is no water.

Duplicating these conditions in the aquarium is not a very difficult matter. Most breeders make a mat of spawning-grass on the bottom. Some use peat-moss with equally good results. Every week or so the eggs are

– *Aphyosemion cognatum. Photo: H. Abel.*

— The Blue Gularis, Aphyosemion sjoestedti, *is a very large and spectacular* Aphyosemion *that reaches a length of about six inches!. Photo: J. Scheel.*

separated from the spawning medium and placed in slightly damp (but not wet) peat-moss. After about 4 weeks the first eggs may be put back in water, and there should be some hatchings. The unhatched eggs may then be returned to the peat moss and the process repeated each week. As with the top-spawners, the fry should be sorted regularly to prevent cannibalism. As may be suspected, the youngsters grow with amazing speed, a highly necessary thing for a fish with such a short life span.

The Blue Gularis, the Yellow Gularis and the Golden Pheasant Fundulus form an intermediate link between the bottom-spawning "annuals" and the top-spawners. Their eggs undergo a long incubation period (up to 6 months), but do not require a period of desiccation.

Most commercial fish breeders who wish to produce top-spawners in quantity use a very efficient system that does away with most of the work required when plants are used as a spawning medium. They make a fat tassel of green nylon yarn by tying a number of threads to a piece of cork. The fish accept this as a plant and spawn into it. The spawning mops, as they are called, are simple to lift out and examine for eggs. When a week or so has gone by, the eggs are removed from the mop to be

– Some killies spawn in the substrate, burying their eggs in sand, gravel, or peat. Shown is a pair of Aphyosemion filamentosum *preparing to spawn in the gravel. Photo: V Elek.*

transferred to the hatching container, or better yet the entire mop is transferred. If the excess water is gently squeezed from the mop, the eggs become clearly visible.

Perhaps some day the interchange of eggs among hobbyists the world over will stimulate a greater appreciation of the beautiful Killifishes and bring the prices down to a level where people are willing to overlook their short life span and keep them anyway for their great beauty, not to mention the ease with which they are maintained and bred. Most of these lovely

— An unusually striking killifish is Aphyosemion striatum, *with blazing neon–red striping on a green background. Such species are always in demand by killie fanciers. Photo: H.–J. Richter.*

fishes, with the exception of the larger species, take well to life in a community aquarium, where pairs are frequently seen to spawn among the plants. Of course, we cannot expect to save many eggs produced in this manner. The Aphyosemions are not very likely to eat their own eggs unless very hungry, but other fishes look upon them as the most delectable sort of food and very few are left after their depredations.

While the *Aphyosemion* species are excellent fishes for the hobbyist who wants to spawn and raise some fry, the professional breeders who produce thousands of other fishes in their hatcheries

— Aphyosemion gardneri. Photo: J. Huber.

— *The Saberfin Killie was until very recently known as* Austrofundulus dolichopterus, *but it is now placed in the genus* Cynolebias. *Photo: H.–J. Richter.*

do not want much to do with them. "Too much handling," they say. If the youngsters are not sorted and separated frequently, the smaller ones keep disappearing and only a few mature fish will result. In order to show a profit, the breeder must charge a high price and if he has to hold his stock for any length of time they soon live out their short life-spans and die, representing a total loss to the breeder for their upkeep and trouble. The same time and trouble spent with the more prolific fishes (like the Barbs, Cichlids or Tetras) results in a quicker and bigger profit.

For this reason many of these somewhat ephemeral beauties are bred by people who are essentially hobbyists but sell their surplus stock to make their fishes pay for their support.

Nothobranchius and Cynolebias

While most of the *Aphyosemion* species are more or less confined to the West African coastal regions, there is another group found along the coastal regions in the eastern part of that highly interesting continent. Some of these bottom-spawning fishes are among the most brilliantly colored of all freshwater species. Gaudiest of these is Rachow's Nothobranchius, *Nothobranchius rachovi.* From Kenya and Tanganyika, along the eastern coast of Africa, we find *Nothobranchius guentheri,* another brilliant beauty, and *Nothobranchius orthonotus,* which occurs a little to the north of this region. All of the *Nothobranchius* species are bottom-spawning "annual" fishes, whose eggs must be partially dried out for a period of at least four weeks before they can be replaced in water to hatch.

It must not be assumed that all of the annual fishes come from Africa. There are also some fishes in South America which share these strange living habits because their pools dry out each year during the dry season. These are the *Cynolebias* species from southern Brazil to Argentina, the *Pterolebias* species from the upper Amazon River region, and the *Rachovia* species from Colombia.

Cynolebias adloffi comes from the southeastern corner of Brazil, where the elimination of swamplands by filling in and the pollution of ponds, pools and ditches by spraying them with oil is reducing this lovely fish to a state of near extinction. There, as in Africa, is a similar contrast of seasons. In the rainy season there are numerous small bodies of water, many of them teeming with fish life. The young fish grow up quickly and spawn copiously into the bottom mud before the dry season overtakes them and brings their inevitable death. Then comes the long but necessary "waiting period" until

– The interesting and rare Aphyosemion exiguum. *Photo: J. Scheel.*

the heavy rains come to refill the pools and release them from their imprisonment. The mortality rate must be a very high one among these eggs. If they are laid in a place where the mud dries out too much, the tiny embryo in the egg dies. The same thing happens when the eggs are laid in a spot where they do not undergo the drying period for a time that is long enough for the embryo to undergo the necessary drying-out stage. Add to this the depredations by other fishes, birds and the like. Probably only one egg out of a hundred ever grows up to be a mature fish, and

– Probably the most interesting killifishes of all are the annuals of the genus Nothobranchius. *This is the Fire Killie,* N. rachovi. *Photo: H. Richter.*

Rockwork is nicely blended with plants in this aquarium designed to serve as a community tank; notice that an unobstructed swimming area is left at the front.

it is one of the wonders of nature that there are any survivors, but these fish have been living for tens of thousands of years in spite of everything, until man comes along and decides to extend the boundaries of his growing cities. He drains the water from the swamps and fills in these areas to make way for buildings and highways. If in the process millions of fish are lost forever, so what? This is just one more proof that man is the worst predator on the face of the earth. The extinction and near extinction of many creatures from the earth is the direct result of man's wanton destruction. Examples are the huge slaughters which led to extinction of Passenger Pigeons in our own United States, and the extinction of the Dodo Birds on the island of Mauritius, where their clumsiness made it an easy matter for a man to overtake them and club them to death.

How many fishes will share this fate is anyone's guess.

A beauty which come to us from Colombia in South America is *Rachovia brevis*. The probability is that the period of seasonal dryness is shorter where this fish is found, because the eggs require only a two-week period of almost total desiccation before they are replaced into the water to hatch. Just the same, the fish has a short life and any specimen that manages to live a whole year may be considered as a sort of Methuselah. As with the others, Mother Nature was lavish with her paint-pot as far as the males were concerned. The males have a brownish back, greenish-blue sides and yellow belly. The dorsal and anal fins are bright blue, and all the scales have blue tips. The tail is grayish with green dots, and the tips of the upper and lower elongated rays are pink. In contrast to this, the females are almost without any color whatsoever, being very small (half the size of the male), and of dull gray coloration.

Panchax

When we mentioned the top-spawning *Aphyosemion* species, it should not be assumed that they are the only top-spawners in Africa; there is another small group native mostly to the western side of this continent, the genus *Epiplatys*. These differ from the *Aphyosemion* genus by having rather flattened heads. They resemble our well-known Pike in appearance as well as habits. They are predators, spending most of their time at or near the surface. Their sharp eyes are forever on alert for anything that moves and can be swallowed.

They are good jumpers, and flying insects doubtlessly form a good part of their diet in their native waters. For this reason their aquarium should be kept covered at all times to prevent them from jumping out of the tank.

Largest of the group for the aquarist is the Banded Panchax, *Epiplatys fasciolatus*. They are easily kept and spawned in the manner of the top-spawning *Aphyosemion* species. A very popular member of the genus is the Fire-Mouth Panchax, *Epiplatys dageti*. Its black bands and startlingly red lower chin make recognition of the males easy. The females lack the red color in the chin. It frequently happens with this species that repeated spawnings will result in a preponderance of females to the extent of as much as six to one. Eggs are deposited on plants near the surface and hatch in approximately two weeks, depending upon the temperature of the water.

There are some Killifishes

-- *Male killies are very territorial and will fight vigorously if permitted. Shown are two male* Nothobranchius patrizii *squaring off for battle, the dominant fish with fins flared threateningly. Photo: K. Tenaka.*

— The Clown Killie (Epiplatys annulatus) is a small delicate species from Sierra Leone and Liberia. This pair is in the act of spawning. The male is the more colorful fish behind the female. Photo: H.-J. Richter.

which are native to the Indian area. These are the *Aplocheilus* species, and have a great similarity to the African *Epiplatys* species in appearance and living habits.

One of these is *Aplocheilus dayi,* the Ceylon Killifish. It is known only from the island of Ceylon and grows to a size of three and one half inches. Not a very active fish, they are frequently content to lie for hours at a time in the shadow of a broad leaf, poised to spring out at anything edible that may happen along. They can move very swiftly and jump considerable distances when the occasion demands, and their tank must be tightly covered.

Smallest of the group is the Dwarf Panchax, *Aplocheilus blocki.* This is a very hardy and attractive species, but because of its size it should be kept with other small fishes only. A very attractive spawner, it can usually be counted upon to lay eggs when conditions are anywhere near right. This fish is available all too rarely in the tanks of dealers. It is not only a beauty in appearance, but is harmless to any fish it cannot swallow.

The largest and probably the most popular species of this group is the Panchax Lineatus, *Aplocheilus lineatus.* This one is apt to be a bit "bossy" in mixed company, and must sometimes be kept where it cannot annoy other fishes. It can account for the disappearance of a smaller fish, like, for instance, a Neon Tetra. Its mouth is large and swallowing ability almost unbelievable. Sometimes one can see a Panchax Lineatus swimming about with the tail of another fish which it has swallowed but cannot get down completely, sticking out of its mouth for about a half hour until it goes all the way down. No fear of its choking.

Rivulus and Jordanella

The Central American countries, as well as South America, contain still another Killifish group, the

Rivulus and Jordanella

Rivulus species. Many of these fishes have a rather unusual marking. Females have a dark, ocellated spot in the upper half of the tail base. Disparity in color between males and females is frequently not as pronounced as with the other Killifishes.

First of these is the Herringbone Rivulus, *Rivulus strigatus,* native to the Amazon Basin. This fish is a bit delicate, and there is generally a majority of males among the tank-raised fry. This is a shy fish which does better in a tank of its own.

The Ocellated Rivulus, *Rivulus ocellatus,* comes from southeastern Brazil. It is not a highly-colored fish, but far from unattractive. The *Rivulus* species spawn like the other top-spawning Killifish species and their eggs hatch in just about the same time.

Dorn's Rivulus, *Rivulus dorni,* comes from the area around Rio de Janeiro. Females lack the usual *Rivulus* spot, but her paler colors make distinguishing her easy.

The Golden Rivulus, *Rivulus urophthalmus,* is normally a fish which is green with red spots on its sides in rows, but sometimes a golden "sport" shows up, which breeders pounce upon and propagate. Thus we often see the gold ones and seldom the green ones.

From Florida comes *Jordanella floridae,* the American Flagfish. This fish is a bit aggressive for mixed company and should have its own aquarium. It should also be offered some vegetable substances in its diet. A pair which is ready to spawn will dig a hole in the gravel and lay eggs in it. The male will then fan and guard the eggs and fry until they are swimming freely. Then the parents should be removed to prevent them from making a meal of their young. American Flagfish require a good-sized tank which is well planted for their well-being.

+ *Although killifishes are usually considered specialty items and are not stocked regularly in many pet shops,* Aplocheilus lineatus, *the Striped Panchax, is an exception—this species is often seen for sale. Photo: B. Kahl.*

— Rivulus holmiae. *Photo: R. Zukal.*

— Rivulus magdalenae. *Photo: R. Zukal.*

— *The Florida Flag Fish* (Jordanella floridae) *may be a bit aggressive toward other fishes so are best kept by themselves. The male of this pair is the lower fish. Photo: H.-J. Richter.*

The young will pick busily at algae and grow well if fed generously on brine shrimp. Like many of our native fishes they are popular in Europe but there is seldom a demand for them in the U.S.A. and dealers know that customers will lose their admiration for them once they find out that they do not come from Africa, Australia or India.

Suggested Reading

ENCYCLOPEDIA OF TROPICAL FISHES by Dr. Herbert R. Axelrod and William Vorderwinkler
ISBN 0-86622-052-6 (H-1077)
Hard Cover, 8½ x 11"; 784 pages.
The world's biggest tropical fish book! Contains over 4000 full-color photos.

ENCYCLOPEDIA OF TROPICAL FISHES by Dr. Herbert R. Axelrod and William Vorkerwinkler
ISBN 0-87666-158-4 (H-905):
Hard cover 5½ x 8"; 631 pages.
Primarily about breeding fishes, but contains plenty of other information as well.

HANDBOOK OF TROPICAL AQUARIUM FISHES (New Edition) by Drs. Herbert R. Axelrod and Leonard P. Schultz
ISBN 0-87666-491-5 (PS-663)
Hard cover, 5½ x 8"; 736 pages. A classic!

EXOTIC TROPICAL FISHES (Original Edition) by Dr. Herbert R. Axelrod, Dr. Cliff W. Emmens, Dr. Duncan Sculthorpe, Mr. William Vorderwinker, Mr. Neal Pronek, and Dr. Warren E. Burgess.
Non-looseleaf hard cover
ISBN 0-87666-051-0 (H-907);
Hard Cover looseleaf (ISBN 0-87666-052-9) (H-907L) 5½ x 8"; 868 pages.
The old standby—the tropical fish field's most sought after book.

EXOTIC TROPICAL FISHES (Expanded Edition) by Dr. Herbert R. Axelrod, Dr. Cliff W. Emmens, Dr. Warren E. Burgess, and Mr. Neal Pronek.
Non-looseleaf hard cover
ISBN 0-87666-543-1 (H-1028);
Looseleaf hard cover ISBN 0-87666-537-7 (H-1028L). An updated and enlarged version of the original.

An aquarium set into a wall immediately becomes the focal point of attention in the room housing it.

A community aquarium set up like this can be beautiful but is exposed to danger of breakage by virtue of having all of its sides exposed to moving traffic in the room.

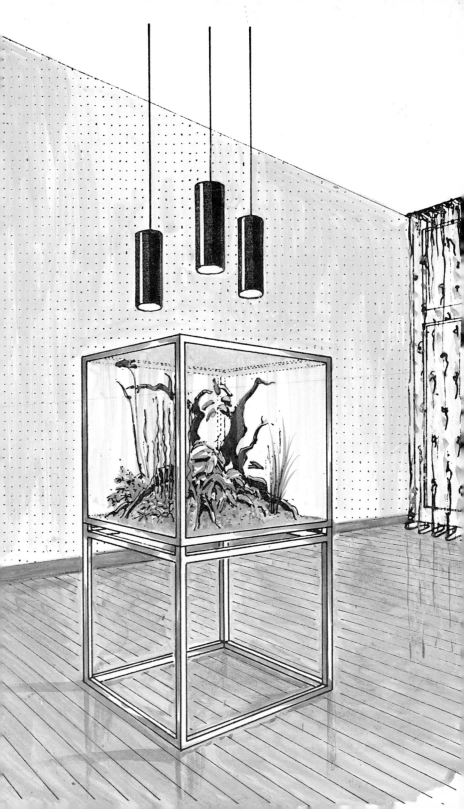

Index

124

125

Cardinal tetras, *Paracheirodon axelrodi*. Photo by B. Kahl.

A COMPLETE INTRODUCTION TO

COMMUNITY AQUARIUMS

COMPLETELY ILLUSTRATED IN FULL COLOR

A well planted and decorated aquarium housing a community of fishes can add a beautiful decorative accent to any home. Photo courtesy of Werther Paccagnella.